SHOEING FOR PERFORMANCE

SHOEING FOR PERFORMANCE

in the Sound and Lame Horse

Haydn Price & Rod Fisher

Trafalgar Square Publishing

NORTH POMFRET, VERMONT

First published in Great Britain in 1989
by The Crowood Press

**First published in the United States of America in 1989
by Trafalgar Square Publishing, North Pomfret, Vermont 05053.**

Library of Congress Catalog Number 88-51356

ISBN   0 943955 14 9

Acknowledgements

All photographs by Haydn Price and Rod Fisher, except those on
pages 30 and 70, by Gillian Greet.

The authors wish to thank Douglas Bradbury, Martin Lewis and
Lorraine Morgan for their photographic assistance and Alan Bailey for
his help and advice in the early stages.

Line-Drawings by Elaine How.

Typeset by Alacrity Phototypesetters, Weston-super-Mare
Printed in Great Britain by The Bath Press

Contents

Foreword

The working relationship between veterinary surgeons and farriers has, in the past, had its difficulties. The two professions were conceived by animal welfare and were originally as one. Farriers of yesteryear were the 'horse doctors' treating sickness and disease. Veterinary surgeons came of age when cruelty to animals was the accepted result of ignorance.

Teaching of foot management at all levels – pony club, horse society, farriery apprentices and veterinary students – has been based on traditional and often limited knowledge, otherwise known as 'perpetual ignorance'. More recently, research programmes into the mechanics of the lower limb and the anatomy and physiology of the foot, have been conducted in various parts of the world. Each community has a style of shoeing suitable to the requirements of their horse power. In most areas of Great Britain, the sporting horse, with great demands on its athleticism, has superseded the working animal. The various activities of horses in sport are mainly spin-offs closely associated with hunting. The snug fit of the hunter shoe, emulated in most disciplines, has been abused by farriers, owners and trainers alike, offering little or no support to the heels. Consequently, many of our horses suffer from collapsed heels – the very area nature intended as a support superstructure. Thin, flat soles are often a direct result of this man-made feature.

Feet, as with other conformation considerations and faults are in-bred natural attributes – native breeds, such as Exmoors, Dartmoor and Fell ponies, have hard horn and deeply-vaulted soles. Consider then, the plight of our 'designer' horses, either long-legged with thin skin and flimsy flat feet, or vastly overweight, again causing the hoof capsule to collapse. Inevitably the sole becomes flat, then the animal is used for producing the next generation!

Would you consider it possible to extend your horse's useful working life by five years? The answer could be yes, if you pay meticulous attention to that part of your beast you may have taken for granted – its feet. Relate them closely to the leg and in turn, the whole limb, the demands of nature and results of domestication. The desire for athletic performance requires perfect timing, balance and co-ordination of the quadruped. Conformational defects will always pose problems, but given sound limbs and feet and the opportunity to service and maintain them, your animal can be fine-tuned by the professionals.

Rod Fisher is a veterinary surgeon with a very practical approach towards farriers and horse shoeing. He has complemented the work of Haydn Price, a young farrier from South Wales, who is a progressive businessman and highly competent craftsman. Both are knowledgeable horsemen and regular riders. This partnership has produced a book with a logical approach to foot problems, and an insight into how to avoid them.

Careful evaluation of the research work, plus extensive 'hands-on' experience, has earned the authors this opportunity to offer sensible considerations in hoof welfare with mechanical implications and therapeutic reasoning. The content represents some of the best ideas incorporated into modern shoeing techniques and indicates the benefits of the improving relationship between the veterinarian, the farrier, the owner and of course, of paramount importance – the horse!

Introduction

All too often there is conflict between the horse owner, the veterinary surgeon and the farrier over the manner in which a horse or pony is being shod. This conflict results from a lack of understanding and communication between the parties involved and a failure by one or more to respect the skills and abilities of the others. The horse owner brands his farrier as incompetent because the farrier leaves the shoes too long in preference to tucking them neatly under the horse's hoof.

'Does the farrier not realise', he asks, 'that this is a recipe for the horse pulling off his shoes?' Unfortunately it has not been explained to the owner that by not fully supporting the heels they will, in the long term, collapse and contract inwards, thereby compressing the structures within. This is the ideal scenario for navicular disease to develop, which is far more serious in the long term than the unlikely possibility of the properly-nailed-on shoe being pulled off. Similarly, the farrier visits a lame horse convinced that he, in handling the feet of horses every day of his working life, knows more than anybody (including the veterinary surgeon) about the foot of

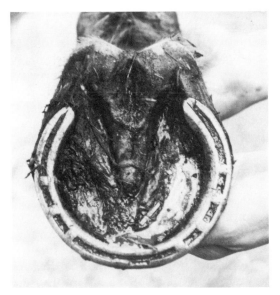

Fig 1 *Inadequate length of shoe at the heels is often believed to reduce the risk of the shoe being torn off.*

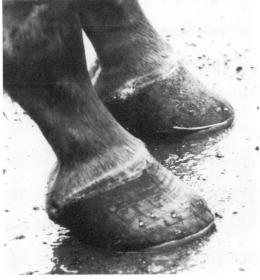

Fig 2 *Over a prolonged period, inadequate support at the heels leads to their collapse.*

the horse. At the same time the veterinary surgeon, with his superior grounding in diseases of the horse and the knowledge to correct them, is convinced that he is the person to sort out the problem. In fact all parties have an important role and all are necessary. If the owner is not prepared to undertake what can sometimes be extensive nursing care then it is often better not to start treatment.

For many years the mutual abuse in the absence of the third person has continued and little attempt has been made on any part to understand and to respect the other's point of view.

Farriery as we know it, in which nails are used to attach a metal protection to the hoof wall, was developed in Roman times. This had certain advantages over attaching a protective pad with leather thongs, but it also brought problems, some of which are with us to this day. It is interesting that the wheel is turning full circle and shoes are now manufactured commercially which are glued to the hoof wall.

Farriery has been officially recognised as a profession since 1356 but it was not until 1975 that legislation was introduced requiring all farriers to be registered. Furthermore, it required that before they could be registered, farriers must obtain qualification by successfully completing a period of apprenticeship with an approved farrier, and secure a Diploma of the Worshipful Company of Farriers. Periods of residential training at a recognised School of Farriery provided the apprentice with a considerably higher standard of theoretical education than had hitherto been possible. In raising his own standard of education he became a far more capable farrier, able to understand more completely the vital prin-

ciples underlying the practical skills of his profession. At the same time he became better able to understand the limitations of his own ability and the areas in which his veterinary colleagues had greater knowledge and ability. Accordingly, the veterinary surgeon recognised a more capable person with greater ability to adapt to the situation. As a result, co-operation between farrier, veterinary surgeon and owner has increased dramatically, which must be beneficial to all parties concerned, but especially to the horse.

Current advances are rapid in the study of new techniques in the preparation of feet and the making and fitting of shoes. These advances are complemented by a similar increase in emphasis on the science part of the art and science of veterinary medicine and surgery. Unfortunately this progress is relayed piecemeal to the horse owner. The more perceptive owner will rapidly grasp the basic principles of shoeing the normal horse and how to avoid problems which may result in lameness. There is, however, a dearth of information available to provide a full explanation of the modern concepts of shoeing the normal horse and the manner in which good farriery can be used to help to correct any problems or, indeed, to explain which problems may arise as a result of bad shoeing and which may not. It is not uncommon, for example, for a horse to become acutely lame on the day after being shod, and for pus to be drained from under the sole of the foot. It is not unusual or unreasonable at first sight to assume that the farrier is to blame. However, such a formation of pus would not form within 24 hours and a more reasonable explanation is that an infection was developing at the time

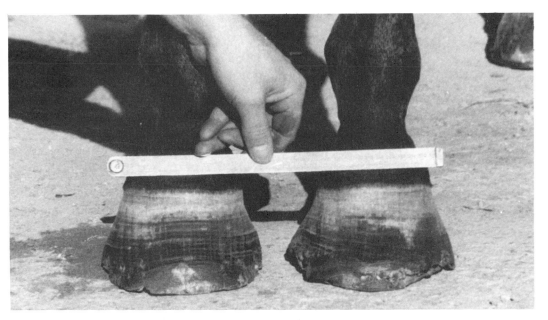

Fig 3   Severe distortion of the foot requires co-operation between farrier, veterinary surgeon and owner to be corrected successfully.

Fig 4   Chronic laminitis cases are a particularly good example of feet that require full co-operation for correction.

that the horse was being shod. Coincidentally, or as the result of normal manipulation of the foot by the farrier, the infection progresses to produce a sudden onset of lameness. The well-informed horse owner will know that such an episode required four to five days to develop and that the farrier cannot be at fault.

The purpose of this book is to provide such information so that the owner is better able to understand the reason why the horse is shod in the manner in which it is, and the problems and pitfalls that may occur in attempting to keep a horse sound. In addition, we shall look at lameness in the lower limb and examine ways in which the farrier's expertise can be used to correct the lameness, or at least to make the lame horse more comfortable.

Horses are not all shod in an identical

manner; many variations are adopted depending on the state of the hoof and the use for which the horse is intended. Further adaptations have been developed to help counteract problems which may have arisen in other parts of the limbs and which are causing lameness. Through this book, the horse owner will better understand the importance of summoning expert professional help as soon as a problem arises.

It is important to understand the extent to which improper shoeing creates or exaggerates disorders of the musculo-skeletal system. Farriery is an art developed over a period of time but based on sound scientific principles, chiefly of mechanics. When the principles are wrongly applied or not adhered to, untold damage can be done. Surprisingly, it is often the mistakes that appear at first glance to be innocuous that cause more insidious damage and are the most serious in the long term. Damage that is inflicted over a long period takes a long period to correct if, indeed, it can ever be corrected. Such damage usually results from failure to correctly balance the foot so that stresses and strains within and around the joints of the limb are not even and the flight path of the limb during movement is altered. Inevitably, any changes to correct such abnormalities must also be made slowly, each situation being judged individually on its merits and requiring all the skill and experience of the farrier.

1 Anatomy and Functional Physiology of the Limbs

It is outside the scope of this book to study the detailed anatomy of the horse, but a basic working knowledge of the more important anatomical features of the limbs and their function is essential.

The skeleton is divided into three areas:

1. The axial skeleton, comprising the skull, spine and the other bones of the chest.
2. The appendicular skeleton, including the bones of the limbs.
3. The splanchnic skeleton, comprising pieces of bone or cartilage that stiffen soft tissue organs of the body.

We will confine our study to the appendicular skeleton. Bone is not an inactive dead substance which never changes its properties, but is continuously being removed and replaced. It is extremely hard, having a high mineral content mixed with carbohydrate and protein. The high calcium content of the bone (more than twice the level of phosphorus) is essential to ensure bone hardness. When the calcium level is reduced compared with the phosphorus level, the bone will become soft and may swell. Horses fed on a diet that is high in phosphorus and low in calcium may develop weakening, softening and swelling of the bones. This will be most obvious in the young horse where new bone is being produced at a great rate.

The level of calcium in the blood is maintained as long as possible while that in bone acts as a reservoir and suffers at a relatively early stage. Certain foods, notably bran but, to a lesser extent, all cereals, contain a high level of phosphorus compared with calcium. When these are fed, a calcium supplement such as ground limestone should be added to the feed.

The bones are responsible for supporting the entire weight of the horse and so need to be very strong. To achieve maximum mechanical strength for weight-bearing, while keeping the weight of bone to a minimum, the primary shape of the bone is that of a cylinder. In the centre is a delicate network of cancellous bone, in the spaces of which bone marrow is found. Bone marrow produces blood cells in the young horse, and stores fat in older horses. The greatest strength would be achieved by having a bony cylindrical column at each corner of the horse. If this were the case, however, the entire concussive force produced when the foot hit the ground would be absorbed through the joints, making movement extremely uncomfortable and damaging the joint excessively. In order to avoid this, in each leg there are points where the limb bends at a joint which acts as a shock absorber. These are the shoulder, elbow and fetlock in the forelimb and hip, stifle, hock and fetlock in the hind limb. Horses

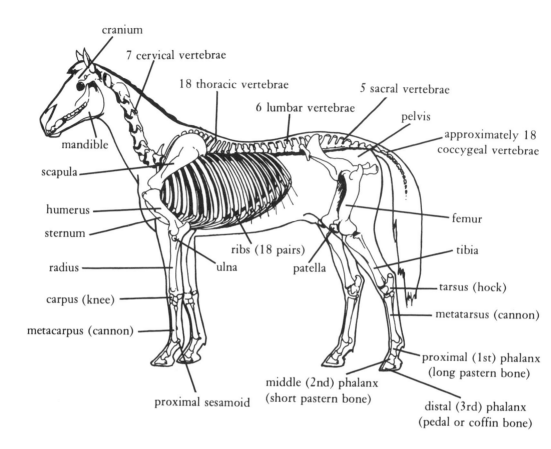

cranium

7 cervical vertebrae

18 thoracic vertebrae

6 lumbar vertebrae

5 sacral vertebrae

pelvis

approximately 18 coccygeal vertebrae

mandible

scapula

humerus

sternum

radius

carpus (knee)

metacarpus (cannon)

ribs (18 pairs)

ulna

patella

femur

tibia

tarsus (hock)

metatarsus (cannon)

proximal (1st) phalanx (long pastern bone)

middle (2nd) phalanx (short pastern bone)

proximal sesamoid

distal (3rd) phalanx (pedal or coffin bone)

Fig 5   Skeleton of horse

that have a conformation which is too upright are predisposed to concussive injuries such as ringbone in the forelimb and bog spavin in the hind limb.

The nutritional supply to bones comes from tiny blood-vessels running in the thin skin-like periosteum that covers the surface of all bones, apart from when the surface is covered by cartilage at a joint, or where tendons or ligaments attach. A dense outer layer protects a highly cellular layer which contains many small blood-vessels and is responsible for producing new bone. A blow to the bone causes a severe reaction in the deeper layer of the periosteum, which

results in a hard bony swelling being produced. Over a period of months the swelling reduces but some form of enlargement may be present indefinitely. The tiny blood-vessels supply nutrients to the outer layers of compact bone. In larger bones a medullary artery passes through a small hole or nutrient foramen into the centre of the bone, where it supplies the bone marrow. The blood-vessels are accompanied by nerves.

The long bones do not grow uniformly from all surfaces but increase in length at certain points – the epiphyses. In the long bones these epiphyses are usually situated towards each end of the bone, just before the articular surface. They are composed of cartilaginous cells which are continuously dividing so that as they age they are moved in each direction along the bone. As this happens they become hard and bony, thus increasing the length of the bone. At a predetermined age the division of cartilage cells stops and no further bone growth occurs. The plate becomes thinner and disappears as growth slows and ceases. The timing of this closure occurs well before the radiographic changes occur on which most data is based. It has an important influence on the time at which corrective surgery for deformities of limbs is carried out.

The bone grows in width by adding new layers of bone to the outside of the shaft while simultaneously removing bone from the inside, thereby preventing the bone from becoming unduly thick.

The Bones of the Foreleg

Unlike the typical mammalian limb as of the dog, for example, the weight of the horse is supported on a single bony column abutting a large scapula or shoulder blade. The thorax of the horse is not attached to the scapula but is slung between the two scapulae in a muscular sling. The humerus is a large dense bone running obliquely back along the lower chest wall from the point of the shoulder to the point of the elbow, heavily protected by muscle. The joint at the shoulder resembles a ball inserted into a socket on the scapula, supported by ligaments. At the elbow a hinged arrangement attaches the humerus to the radius and ulna bones. The ulna forms the point of the elbow or olecranon and tapers down the back of the forearm where it joins the radius. The radius runs vertically to the knee and supports all the weight. At the knee a series of seven or eight bones are arranged as a top row of three bones with a fourth, accessory carpal bone, behind. Below is a second row of four bones, of which the first carpal bone may be absent. These bones allow movement between the radius and the top (proximal) row of carpal bones.

The single column of bones beneath the knee is all that is left of the original five columns of the mammalian limb, and represents the third, or middle, digit. The large metacarpal or cannon bone transmits forces vertically downward to the fetlock. Being long and slender and largely unprotected, it is very vulnerable to injury. The bone is oval from side to side in cross-section and immensely strong for its size. Its flattened posterior surface helps to protect the suspensory ligament and flexor tendons which provide support to the lower limb. This protection is increased by two small metacarpal or splint bones which taper as they run, one down each side of the lateral aspect of the cannon bone, outside the suspensory ligament. They are all that remains of the second and fourth digits and are closely attached to the cannon bone by a fibrous attachment (the interosseous ligament), in the young horse. At about five years of age the interosseous ligament becomes bony so that the two bones fuse.

The splint bones are triangular in shape below the knee and extend approximately two-thirds of the way down the cannon bone, ending in a button-like enlargement at the distal (bottom) extremity. This enlargement may stand clear of the cannon bone and may be mistaken for a

15

splint. The cannon bone has a ridged distal extremity, dividing it into two articular surfaces and preventing any rotational movement in the fetlock.

At the fetlock most of the weight of the horse is transmitted downwards and forwards through the long pastern bone (proximal or first phalanx). At the back of the joint two small pyramidal bones (the proximal sesamoid bones), are present, one on each side of the distal cannon bone. They are closely attached to the joint by ligaments and act as a pulley around which the deep digital flexor tendon passes as it changes its direction and runs to the solar aspect of the pedal bone (third phalanx). When the deep digital flexor tendon changes direction again, this time to pass over the coffin (distal interphalangeal) joint, another sesamoid bone, the navicular bone, is present to act as another pulley. The proximal sesamoid bones are attached by ligaments to the distal border of the cannon bone and the proximal border of the first phalanx. These bones increase the working surface of the fetlock joint and provide an anchor for the suspensory ligament.

The digit comprises three weight-supporting bones – the phalanges – and the distal sesamoid bone. The first phalanx is relatively long, with a waist. It runs obliquely forwards and downwards at approximately 55 degrees to the horizontal from the fetlock. Variation of this angle dictates whether excessive concussive forces are passed through the joints of the digit (as happens if the bone is too upright), or excessive strain is placed on the tendons and ligaments behind the fetlock (as happens if the bone is too sloping).

The second phalanx or short pastern

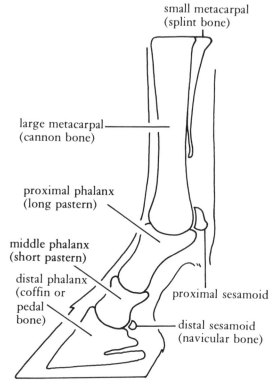

Fig 6   *Bony anatomy of lower limb (lateral view).*

bone is squat and solid in structure. It continues the line of slope of the pastern, running to the pedal bone.

The pedal bone or third phalanx is situated entirely within the hoof. Viewed from the side it is triangular in shape with a large cartilaginous plate on the upper surface of the wing on each side of the bone. When this plate becomes bony, which is a normal feature of ageing, it is known as a sidebone and may create problems, especially if ossification is rapid and premature. The normal springiness that can be felt above the coronet on each side of the foot is replaced by a hard, unyielding structure.

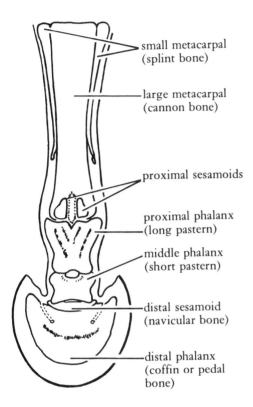

small metacarpal (splint bone)

large metacarpal (cannon bone)

proximal sesamoids

proximal phalanx (long pastern)

middle phalanx (short pastern)

distal sesamoid (navicular bone)

distal phalanx (coffin or pedal bone)

Fig 7   Bony anatomy of lower limb (palmar view).

The anterior surface of the pedal bone supports the sensitive laminae to which the hoof wall is attached. The ventral or ground surface of the bone is concave, producing a vaulted structure that increases its strength. The margin of this surface is not parallel to the ground, but is normally rotated so that the toe is at five degrees to the ground surface. The deep digital flexor tendon attaches to the posterior part of the ground surface of the pedal bone.

Although small and flattened, running across the posterior part of the distal interphalangeal (coffin) joint, the navicular bone is extremely important. It is very susceptible to excessive pressure which may restrict the normal flow of blood to the lower surface of the bone. If blood flow is compromised, the bone starts to disintegrate. It is also susceptible to injury from penetrating objects in the heel area of the frog.

The hind limb is more angled, allowing the joints to be compressed and then to expand with a force that propels the horse forward or upward. Consequently the bulky femur runs obliquely forward from its attachment to the pelvis at the point of the hip, to the stifle. Here it articulates with the tibia which runs back again to the point of the hock. Both bones are heavily surrounded by muscle. The patella or kneecap at the stifle anchors the muscles that extend the stifle joint so that they are carried clear of the joint but are able to fix on to the proximal tibia.

The hock or tarsus acts as a large pulley wheel allowing movement in a hinge-like action. It comprises up to seven bones although some may be fused, allowing forces to be transferred from the tibia to the metatarsus or cannon bone. The bony anatomy of the hind leg below the hock is essentially the same as that of the forelimb below the knee.

All of the joints are supported by a complex arrangement of ligaments that run between adjacent bones, preventing the bones from moving too far in relation to each other. The surfaces of the joints are covered by a smooth layer of cartilage which reduces friction during movement and helps to absorb concussion. This is helped by a watertight capsule surrounding the cartilaginous surfaces which prevents the synovial joint fluid from escaping. The fluid has a sophisticated hydraulic function by which concussion is further reduced. Joint fluid is produced by the capsule itself.

Active movement of the limbs is brought about by the contraction of muscles. To maintain the maximum efficiency, the bulk of the muscle is situated at the top of the limbs, where movement is minimal. The muscles are divided into two major groups, those that extend the leg and a larger group that flex it. The muscles function in conjunction with tendons which extend on the anterior and posterior surfaces of the limbs. The purpose of the extensor muscles and tendons is to straighten the limb in readiness for landing. This is a considerably easier job than that of supporting the weight of the horse by preventing overextension of the joints, a function that is performed by the much larger flexor tendons.

Each leg has two major extensor tendons and two major flexor tendons. The common digital extensor tendon arises from the common digital extensor muscle anchored to the humerus and the radius around the elbow joint. The muscular belly becomes tendon well above the knee. The tendon runs through a synovial sheath on the front of the knee, and over a bursa which acts as a cushion at the fetlock. Finally it attaches to the front of the pedal bone at the top (the extensor process of the proximal dorsal surface of the third phalanx). As it passes over the first phalanx it is joined on each side by branches of the suspensory ligament from the proximal sesamoid bones behind the fetlock joint. The tendon also has smaller attachments to the first two phalanges.

The common digital extensor muscle has the function of flexing the elbow and

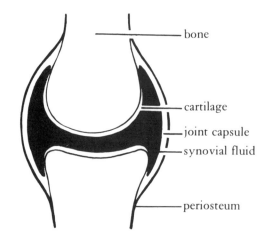

Fig 8   Basic anatomy of a joint.

extending the knee, fetlock and digital joints. The lateral digital extensor muscle is a much smaller muscle which also becomes tendinous above the knee, before running down the outside of the joint and trending towards the front of the fetlock to attach on the anterior surface of the long pastern bone (first phalanx).

In the hind leg the long digital extensor muscle has a similar function to the common digital extensor of the foreleg. The lateral digital extensor merges with it just below the hock joint.

The superficial and deep digital flexor tendons arise from muscles of the same name situated in the muscle mass behind the leg, between the elbow and knee. By the time they reach the posterior surface of the knee and pass through the carpal sheath that holds them close to the knee, they are entirely tendinous. At the fetlock the deep flexor tendon passes

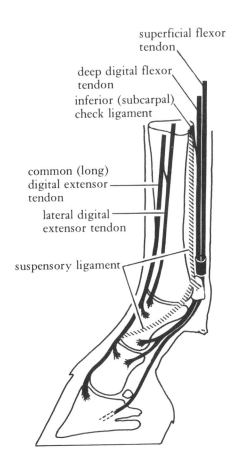

superficial flexor tendon

deep digital flexor tendon

inferior (subcarpal) check ligament

common (long) digital extensor tendon

lateral digital extensor tendon

suspensory ligament

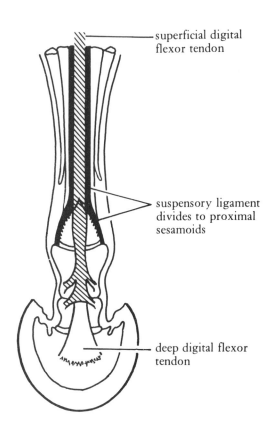

superficial digital flexor tendon

suspensory ligament divides to proximal sesamoids

deep digital flexor tendon

Fig 9   Arrangement of tendons and ligaments in the lower limb (lateral view).

Fig 10   Arrangement of tendons and ligaments in the lower limb (palmar view).

through a ring formed by the superficial tendon and both are attached to the joint by a ligament around the joint. The deep flexor tendon continues and attaches to the solar surface of the pedal bone, after passing over the posterior surface of the navicular bone which acts as a pulley, and fanning out. Another bursa acts as a cushion between tendon and navicular bone. The superficial tendon divides midway down the pastern, the two divisions attaching to the first and second

phalanges behind the collateral ligaments that support the joint.

The arrangement of flexor muscles and tendons of the hind limb is essentially the same as that of the forelimb.

The ligaments that support the back of the knee extend downwards and join the deep digital flexor tendon as the subcarpal (or inferior) check ligament, acting as a stabiliser for the tendon. The tarsal check ligament of the hind limb runs from the posterior surface of the hock joint and

19

has a similar function. Similarly, the superior check ligament in the forelimb attaches the posterior surface of the distal radius to the superficial digital flexor tendon just above the knee.

The task of the flexor tendons is helped by the band of suspensory ligament that runs from its attachment to the posterior surface of the cannon bone immediately below the knee. Just above the fetlock the band divides, one half going to each proximal sesamoid bone, before continuing round the outside of the pastern to attach to the digital extensor tendon on the anterior surface of the pastern.

The Anatomy and Functional Physiology of the Foot

The Hoof Wall

The hoof wall is a very specialised structure, unique in its design. Not only must it carry the weight of the horse but it must also resist wear and absorb concussion, especially when working on hard surfaces. It must also protect the sensitive structures that it encapsulates. The structure of the hoof enables us to extend the capability of the horse for both work and pleasure by the attachment of shoes.

The hoof wall is an extension of the superficial layers of the skin (the epidermis). The coronary band runs horizontally round the top of the hoof wall. It can be likened to the quick of your fingernail, and its appearance resembles velvet, with small teat-like projections called papillae. Each papilla produces a tube or horn which can be clearly seen under a microscope. The tubes are comprised of tubular horn and are bonded together by a sub-

stance called intertubular horn. The horn tubes are spherical in cross section but as the horn is being developed and thickened they become flatter and overlap each other. They also harden by a process called keratinization. The horn tubes have the ability to bend and compress. They can be trained to their correct position and shaped by trimming the feet at the ground surface. The fact that they compress gives them the ability to absorb concussion which is passed vertically up the hoof wall as the horse's weight is applied to the foot. Under normal circumstances it takes between nine and twelve months for the hoof to grow from the coronary band to the ground surface. However, many things affect the growth rate, including the following factors:

1. *Nutrition.* This is a major factor influencing hoof growth rate. Horses that are fed on a good-quality healthy diet have a hoof wall which has a faster growth rate. Likewise, a horse that is turned out on good grazing will benefit from the improved nutritional value of lush grass, provided that it is not eaten in excess! Evidence of this can be clearly seen as growth rings on the hooves of horses which have changed their diet. The rings run horizontally around the hoof. Several such rings should, in the normal horse, be parallel.

Some specific nutritional deficiencies are recognised to cause defects in the formation of the hoof wall. Hooves in which there is an absence of horn in the outer layer respond favourably to dietary supplementation with the vitamin biotin. The hoof wall will have a similar appearance, however, where the organisation of the structure in the centre of the hoof is lost by failure of the keratin cells to stick

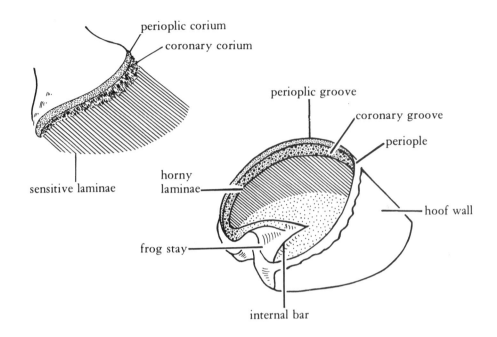

Fig 11   Structure of the hoof capsule.

together. Both conditions are seen as a crumbling of the hoof wall, reduction of the stride length caused by tender feet, and frequent loss of shoes. The latter condition is not, however, affected by dietary biotin levels but improves when protein levels are increased and ground limestone is added to the diet. The effect of the calcium in the ground limestone is to increase the rate of growth of the keratin and to increase the ability of keratin cells to stick together. Occasionally destructive bacteria play a secondary role in damaging hoof wall.

2.   *Ground type.* Environmental conditions have an important effect on the horse's general welfare. In a horse that is stabled, the type of bedding used can affect the growth rate and condition of the hoof. A horse that is kept on wood shavings will usually have a rather dry hard foot. This is due to the shavings 'drawing' the foot to remove the moisture. In addition there is a tendency for the shavings to ball up over the soles of the feet. The compressed shavings then harden the feet. In contrast, the horse on a peat bed would not have such a dry foot since the peat gives a soft, moist substance for the horse to stand on. Similarly, the horse on a hard dried field in summer will develop a dry, flaky sole, while the horse standing for long periods in marshy ground has a hoof that remains soft and pliable.

3.   *Body condition.* Horses in poor bodily condition tend to have poor quality hoof wall as a result of the inadequate nutritional intake.

The weight distribution of the horse is divided so that approximately 60 per cent of the total weight is supported by the forelimbs and 40 per cent by the hind limbs, due to the fact that the entire weight of the head and neck is forward of the forelegs. Thus the chief function of the forelimbs is to carry weight and support the body, whereas the hind limbs are designed for propulsion. The horse is adapted for propulsion by having a large muscular development over the hind quarters. The difference in function of the fore and hind limbs is helped by the difference in shape between the fore and hind feet. The forefeet are rounded in appearance with a flatter sole, distributing weight over a wider area. The hind feet take on a more oval shape so that they do not interfere with each other as they propel the horse forward.

Periople

The outer covering of the horny hoof wall is the periople. It is responsible for

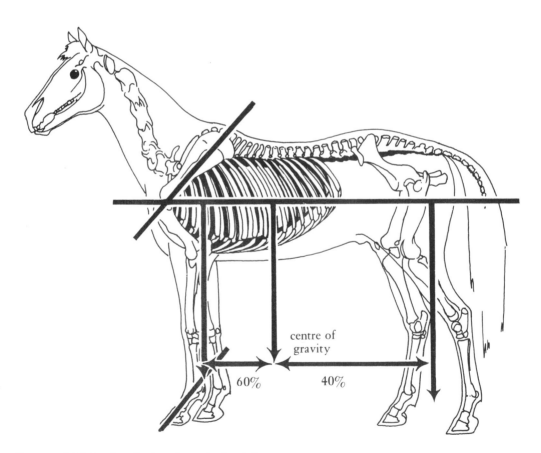

Fig 12   Weight distribution through the skeleton.

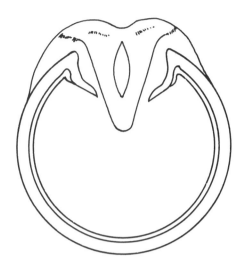

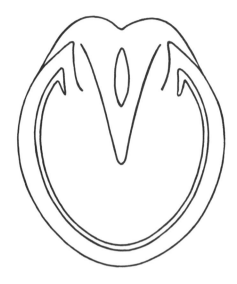

Fig 13   The forefoot (ground surface).

Fig 14   The hind foot (ground surface).

the control of evaporation and moisture content within the foot. Situated as a horizontal band below the coronary band it thickens towards the heels and finally blends with the bulbs of the heels. At its lower margin with the hoof wall it takes on the appearance of varnish and continues approximately two-thirds of the way down the hoof wall. The periople can be most clearly distinguished from the coronary band on those feet that have been subjected to wet conditions as, for example, when a horse is brought in from a field on which a heavy dew is present. The importance of not rasping the outer hoof wall in case the removal of the periople leads to dehydration of the hoof appears to be heavily over-emphasised.

The Bars

At the heels the hoof wall bends sharply forwards and inwards to continue alongside the frog while gradually fading to nothing by the time that it gets halfway to the point of the frog. The bar, as this reflected wall is called, is capable of taking and distributing weight, thereby extending the bearing surface of the foot.

The Sole

The sole covers the majority of the base of the foot. Its main function is to protect the sensitive structures within. Because it is to a greater or lesser extent concave, it has a greater ability to support weight. The development of the sole is similar to that of the wall in that horn tubules grow down from papillae immediately above them across the deeper layer of the sole. One difference in development is that the sole is able to flake away when the horn tubules have gained sufficient length. This flaking is particularly obvious on some horses and is quite normal. Opinion differs regarding whether the sole should be pared during preparation of the foot for shoeing. It is unlikely that where paring is required and is performed, the practice would be detrimental to the foot.

The Frog

The frog is a wedge-shaped mass of horn with a rubbery consistency, situated at the heels and pointing forward into the sole of the foot. Its major function is to support and stabilise the digital cushion, but it also protects the sensitive frog. Furthermore, it helps to prevent the foot from slipping and from becoming contracted at the heels.

The high moisture content of the frog, higher than any other part of the foot, accounts for its soft rubbery texture. In some horses the frog is withdrawn and deep, reflecting the nature of the environment in which the horse is kept. In severe cases contraction of the frog may be followed by contraction of the foot. Ground contact should be possible only in soft going as the frog cuts and sinks into the ground naturally. This is also possible in the shod foot. The frog contracts normally when the foot is lifted. After a shoe has been applied and the toe raised off the ground it is reasonable to assume that the horse would be unable to gain any frog pressure at all. However, in the standing horse the displacement of weight through the foot enables the frog to expand. In other words, in the normal foot the frog does not have to come into contact with the ground to achieve the required frog pressure. Excessive frog pressure can be detrimental to the horse since it can cause over-expansion of the foot.

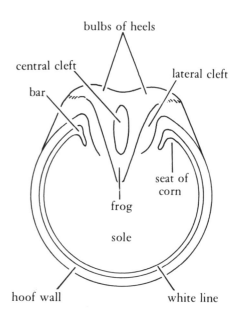

Fig 15   Structures of the ground surface of the foot.

The Digital Cushion and Lateral Cartilages

The physical movements of the foot and the immense pressure caused by the descending body weight against the upward ground pressure necessitate a major absorber of concussion within the foot. The digital cushion fulfills this role. It is situated above the frog within the internal structure of the foot and blends into the bulbs of the heels. The digital cushion is fibro-fatty in composition and is essentially insensitive. This enables it to absorb concussion by being deformed and compressed without feeling pain. When weight is placed on the fetlock, the digital cushion is compressed from above. It is supported and centralised from below by

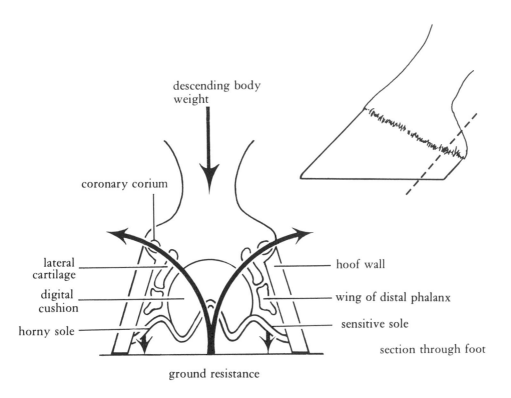

descending body weight

coronary corium

lateral cartilage

digital cushion

horny sole

hoof wall

wing of distal phalanx

sensitive sole

section through foot

ground resistance

Fig 16   Energy dispersal within the foot.

the horny frog. The lines of pressure extend through the frog and obliquely through the digital cushion on to the lateral cartilages of the pedal bone (distal phalanx). This pressure causes the foot to expand at the heel. The lateral cartilages are two wing-like plates of fibrocartilage, one lying vertically on each side of the digital cushion and rising up from the wings of the pedal bone. Approximately one half of the cartilage is contained within the hoof while the other half protrudes above the coronet. The cartilages can be felt in the standing horse and under normal circumstances will yield to thumb pressure. Combined with the effect of the digital cushion, they are able to dissipate the concussive forces through the hoof wall. As the horse ages it is

common for the fibrocartilage to be replaced by bone so that the lateral cartilages lose their elasticity and become rigid, a condition known as 'sidebone'. Either one or both lateral cartilages can be affected. The condition is discussed in further detail in Chapter 7.

White Line

A narrow line situated between the sole and the wall when viewed from the ground surface is known as the 'white line'. It acts as an expansion joint between these two structures and is a useful guide to the thickness of the hoof wall. Under certain circumstances the white line itself may become widened.

25

The Horny Laminae

The entire internal surface of the hoof wall is occupied by small vertical leaves, the horny, non-sensitive laminae. The leaves protrude inwards from the hoof wall, extending vertically downwards from the coronary groove to the ground surface. The primary horny laminae total five to six hundred, and each laminal leaf has one to two hundred secondary laminae which extend at right angles to the primary laminae. The laminae are designed to interdigitate with the sensitive laminae which form a mirror image and which protrude outwards from their attachment with the surface of the pedal bone (distal or third phalanx). The sensitive laminae provide the nutritional supply to the horny laminae.

This unique design enables the hoof wall, which is being constantly produced, to move downwards by allowing the horny laminae to slide over the sensitive laminae. The bond between the two is immensely strong – so strong that if it were possible to remove the sole and supporting structures of the foot there would be no displacement between the horny and sensitive laminae. The nerve supply to the sensitive laminae and the corresponding attachment to the horny

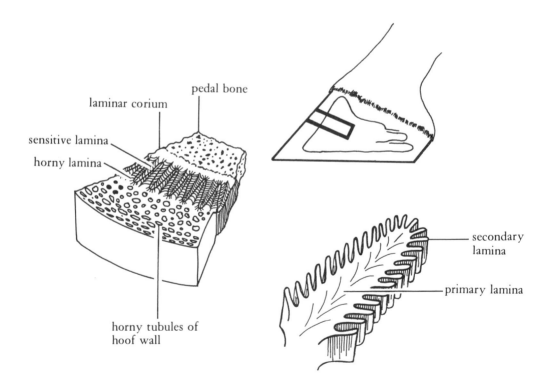

Fig 17 Interaction of the horny and sensitive laminae.

laminae enables the horse to 'feel' with its feet. Consequently it can counteract any changes in underlying ground contours accordingly. Some weight and concussion are absorbed and dissipated through these structures.

The Sensitive Structures of the foot

Every horny structure of the foot has a corresponding sensitive structure. All of the sensitive structures of the foot are situated on the internal aspect of the hoof. They are sensitive because they have a blood and nerve supply. We can therefore assume that any penetration or injury to the structures causes distress to the horse resulting from pain and in some instances loss of blood.

Perioplic corium The perioplic corium is part of the coronary band situated beneath the proximal (top) border of the hoof wall. It is situated in the perioplic groove which widens at the heel and merges with the coronary groove. Starting as a narrow band it extends around the hoof, then widens and blends into the bulbs of the heels, producing the periople. As the perioplic corium widens, it produces a thicker layer of periople which helps to bind the bulbs of the heels and the frog together.

Coronary corium Immediately below the perioplic corium is a wider and thicker band, the coronary corium. It is reflected inwards at the heels to form part of the structure of the bars. The chief function of the coronary corium is in producing the hoof wall, via the papillae. The thickness and depth of the corium are related to the thickness of the hoof wall. It is found to be thickest at the toe, gradually reducing towards the heels. The structure of the corium assists in the dissipation of concussion.

Sensitive laminae (Laminal corium) Situated on the anterior surface of the pedal bone in vertical rows resembling the pages of a book are the sensitive laminae. They arise from the papillae of the laminar corium which extends over the surface of the pedal bone, and lie between the bone and the horny laminae. The fleshy leaf-like projections extend down the entire length of the internal surface of the hoof. Each sensitive lamina has primary and secondary leaves that interlock with their horny counterparts. The horny laminae receive their nutritional supply via the sensitive laminae.

Sensitive sole (Corium of the sole) The sensitive sole covers the ground surface of the third phalanx. It resembles velvet in appearance and is composed of papillae similar to those of the coronary band. It is responsible for providing the nutrient supply to the horny sole that overlies it. The sensitive sole has a major blood supply similar to all of the sensitive structures. If the blood vessels between the sensitive sole and the horny sole become crushed by the shoe at the wings of the pedal bone, bruising, or corns, will arise.

Sensitive frog (Corium of the frog) This extends to cover a portion of the digital cushion at the heels and is called the sensitive frog. It becomes a mirror image of the horny frog and serves to produce horny frog via the papillae. The corium of the frog is thicker than that of the sole. It also provides nutrition to the digital cushion.

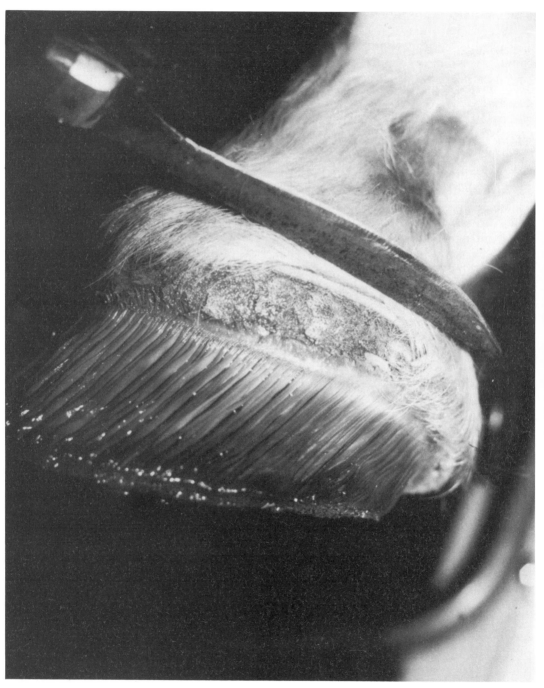

Fig 18   The leaf-like structure of sensitive laminae.

The Blood Supply to the Legs

The blood supply to the foot is split into three component types of vessels: arteries, capillaries and veins. Rich, oxygenated blood is conveyed to the leg and foot via the arterial system. Arteries are thick-walled tubes which are composed of three layers. The outer layer is a soft fibrous skin which covers the muscular middle layer and is lined by a fine membrane which ensures a smooth passage for blood to flow.

The major artery supplying the foreleg is the brachial artery which enters the leg under the shoulder as the axillary artery, giving off branches as it courses along the humerus. It crosses the inside of the elbow joint and becomes the median artery. The pulse can be felt at this point, just below the elbow on the inside of the radius. Midway down the forearm it divides into the radial and ulnar arteries, the former being smaller and deeper. The ulnar artery provides the major supply to the lower limb, but remains in contact with the radial artery by a series of arches from which the metacarpal artery arises.

The arterial blood supply to the hind limb is derived from the aorta running along the midline immediately beneath the lumbar spine. On reaching the pelvis it divides to give two iliac arteries, one supplying each hind leg. Once inside the leg they become femoral arteries. Initially the femoral artery does not run deep, running down the inside of the leg, but lower down the thigh it moves to the outside of the leg and becomes deeper, producing branches all along its route. Becoming the cranial tibial artery it continues deep in the muscle on the anterior aspect of the tibia, until it reaches the hock as the dorsal metatarsal artery.

A single major artery, the metacarpal artery (metatarsal artery in the hind limb), supplies the lower limb. The name is derived from its passage down the metacarpal or cannon bone. The artery can be called the common digital artery in both fore and hind limbs. It runs on the internal (medial) and back (caudal) aspect of the forelimb. In the hind limb it runs on the external (lateral) and caudal aspects of the limb. A small branch supplies the metacarpal bone with blood. Just above the fetlock the artery divides into two digital arteries, one running on the inside (medial) and the other running on the outside (lateral) aspect of the foot, following the margins of the flexor tendons after passing round the outside of their corresponding proximal sesamoid bone. Two small branches leave the main artery, one to supply each of the proximal and second phalangeal bones. At the inner border of the wings of the third phalanx, the medial and lateral digital arteries subdivide once more to become the plantar and pre-plantar arteries. The pre-plantar arteries pass along the pre-plantar groove on each wing of the third phalanx and continue to the anterior surface of the bone where they supply blood to the sensitive laminae.

The plantar arteries run on the inner aspect of the wings of the third phalanx, this time in the plantar groove which carries them to a hole in the solar surface of the bone. Here they rejoin as the terminal arch inside the tip of the bone. Many small branches ramify from the arch inside the bone, extending to the sensitive laminae and the sensitive sole. They also form the artery round the circumference of the bone (the artery of the distal border). It is important to understand that the blood supplies the

29

pedal and navicular bones from their lower surfaces.

The digital arteries can be felt at a point behind the pastern or just above the fetlock. The pulse is increased in speed by a variety of factors including pain, and the character of the pulse changes, becoming fuller, when a disease process is taking place within the foot. By comparing the difference between the character of the medial and lateral digital arteries it is sometimes possible to localise the process to one side of the foot.

Arteries divide and subdivide to become microscopic thin-walled capillaries. These vessels have no muscle in their walls and are consequently unable to change their diameter to redirect the flow of blood as is done by the arterioles. Capillaries are the end blood-vessels which actually carry the nutrients to the living tissues.

De-oxygenated blood is carried by thin-walled veins back to the heart and lungs. A network of small veins or venules forms a plexus to collect the blood. They have no pulse because they have no inherent ability to contract and are too far around the circulatory system to be affected by waves of contraction by the heart, consequently they must rely on compression by the physical movements of the foot and the contraction of adjacent muscles to maintain blood-flow and convey the blood back up the leg. In the upper leg, valves are situated at strategic points within the vein, which prevent backflow so that the blood does not pool under the effects of gravity in the foot and lower leg.

Three major plexuses exist within the foot:

1. The solar plexus is situated within

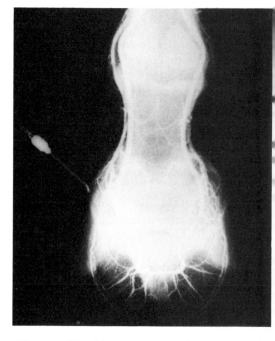

Fig 19   The blood supply to the normal foot.

the sensitive sole on the solar surface of the third phalanx. It is pressurised by compression between the descending body weight and the upward ground resistance. The result is that blood is forced out of the foot.

2. The laminal plexus terminates in the sensitive laminae. The network of veins relies upon the physical movements of the wall in conjunction with the third phalanx to compress the plexus and drain the system to the major veins.

3. Finally, there are two coronary plexuses present, one on each side of the foot, extending above the coronary band and partially covering the lateral cartilage. The expansion and contraction of the foot together with pressure exerted on the lateral cartilage compresses the plexus. Both the medial (inside) and

lateral (outside) plexuses converge like fingers on a hand to join the main veins, the digital veins, which continue upwards, running immediately in front of their corresponding artery. They join just above the fetlock to form the venous arch. The arch supplies three metacarpal veins, which run parallel up the caudal (rear) aspect of the cannon bone. In the hind limbs the vascular arrangement is essentially the same as in the forelimbs.

When filled, the blood vessels within the foot act as a hydraulic system, assisting in absorbing concussion. No major blood vessels are present in or around the frog so that, contrary to popular opinion, the frog does not have a direct pumping action in blood circulation.

The venous drainage of the legs essentially follows the arterial supply. Veins rely on passive action to keep the blood flowing through them. Squeezing from outside by the contraction of adjacent muscles helps to maintain blood flow and prevents congestion in the limbs.

The Nerve Supply to the Legs

Nerves are thin, white cord-like structures originating from the central nervous system of the brain and the spinal cord. The nerve fibres that convey messages to the central system, the afferent fibres, supply information to the brain concerning sensations of touch, pain and pressure. Efferent fibres, on the other hand, are responsible for controlling reactions such as muscle movements and co-ordination.

The nervous supply joins the forelimb at the brachial plexus beneath the shoulder-blade and comprises five spinal nerves. Six major nerves are present in the plexus, each supplying its own area of the limb. A pair of nerves follow the margins of the flexor tendons down the back of the cannon bone, accompanied by the appropriate veins and arteries. They are continuations of the median and ulnar nerves. Midway down the cannon bone a communicating branch runs between the two nerves.

At the level of the fetlock the branches divide to form the digital nerves. The anterior and posterior branches pass to their respective sides of the pedal bone where they ramify and supply the surrounding tissues. A branch off the anterior digital nerve may be one discrete nerve or a series of small nerves forming the middle digital nerve. The anterior nerve supplies the coronary corium, the skin and the common digital extensor tendon which runs to the front of the third phalanx. The middle digital nerve runs to the sensitive laminae and the coronary corium also. The function of the posterior digital nerve is to supply innervation to the sensitive sole, the third phalanx, joints, navicular bone and the sensitive frog.

In the hind limb the lumbosacral plexus at the front of the pelvis is made up from five more pairs of spinal nerves. Again, a series of nerves supply their own specific areas. The most important is the sciatic nerve which runs behind the hip joint, giving off branches on its way to the stifle. It then continues, as the tibial nerve, to divide in two just above the hock. The nerve supply to the lower hind limb is essentially the same as to the forelimb. In this case, however, the plantar nerves that course down the cannon bone to divide into digital nerves are supplied by the tibial nerve.

By infiltrating local anaesthetic around

the nerves at specific points (so-called 'nerve blocks') it is possible to prevent the flow of nerve impulses to and from the area below the point of blocking. Since any pain in the area is removed the lame horse will move more comfortably so that by this response the site of lameness can be localised. This is therefore a useful tool in reaching a diagnosis when the cause of lameness is obscure.

In some cases where a lameness is incurable it has been the practice in the past to permanently eliminate the pain by removing a short section of the nerve to the painful area. This procedure creates many problems since the nerve supply to a series of structures is inevitably destroyed, causing their death. Furthermore, loss of feeling in the foot renders the horse likely to stumble so that it is no longer as safe to ride. These drawbacks, together with considerable recent advances in the treatment of specific conditions of the foot, render the procedure virtually obsolete.

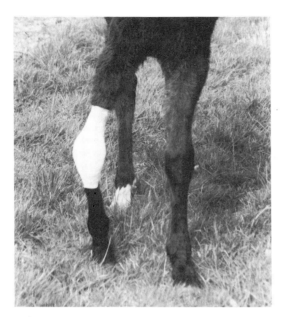

Fig 22   Severe deviation of the forelimb at the distal epiphysis of the radius, just above the knee.

litter and allowed to stand and to walk freely on a firm flat surface, thereby reducing the risk of uneven pressure on the growth plates. This also facilitates viewing of the legs of the animal so that any abnormalities are noticed at an early age. In the more severe cases of limb misalignment in the young animal it may be necessary to interfere surgically to alter the growth rate at the epiphysis.

The traditional method of doing this is to restrict the growth rate on the active side of the plate; that is, on the outside of the curve. A large surgical staple can be placed across the epiphysis but there is a tendency for the ends to be pulled apart by the force of the growing bone. Greater success is usually obtained by placing screws in the bone above and below the plate and joining a surgical wire between them to prevent them from being moved apart. The disadvantages

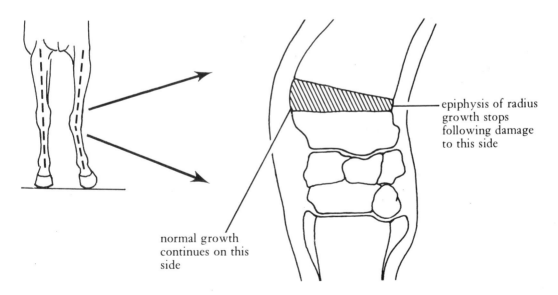

normal growth continues on this side

epiphysis of radius growth stops following damage to this side

Fig 23   Limb deviation at the carpus.

with both of these techniques are two-fold. First it is obviously undesirable, unless absolutely necessary, to introduce artificial materials into the leg. Also, once the leg is straight, the material must be removed or over-correction will take place. A more satisfactory treatment is to increase the growth rate on the inside of the curve. This can be done by surgically cutting and lifting the skin-like periosteum that stretches over the whole bone on that side of the joint. This has the further advantage that once the bone is straightened the correction stops spontaneously.

Conformational Defects of the Fore Limb

Hoof/Pastern Axis

The forelimb is designed as a pillar in order to support the majority of the weight of the horse. The ideal conformation of the limb is such that, when viewed from the front, a straight line can be drawn vertically downwards to bisect the knee through the centre and continue through the centre of the fetlock, pastern and hoof. Viewed from the side, the perpendicular dropped from the point of the shoulder should pass through the centre of the knee and fetlock to the ground. A second line passes from the centre of the fetlock through the centre of the pastern and the hoof, making an angle of 50–55 degrees with the ground surface. This line is known as the hoof/pastern axis and is one of the most important concepts of the correct balancing of the foot.

A horse with the foreleg conformation described is well balanced, with its weight evenly distributed through the column. This ideal is, however, not always possible and any deviation is likely to result in the possibility of interference with the opposite limb and uneven pressure on the cartilage working surfaces of the bones within the joints. A large proportion of lower limb lamenesses, which are themselves the vast majority of all lamenesses, can be directly attributed to conformation. It is therefore essential that the hoof should be trimmed in a manner such that even if it does not correct the fault completely, it at least enables the limb of the horse to operate without interference from other limbs.

One of the most important factors to consider when assessing limb alignment and conformation is the effect of the limb on the horse when it is in motion. The most noticeable effect is that on footfall. This is the moment when the foot comes into contact with the ground. In the shod horse the wear on the used shoe can relate directly to the conformation and any associated problems. If a horse is inclined to land unevenly on his feet this results in uneven wear on the shoe. As a result the joints of the limb are subjected to uneven pressures. It is vital for the correct function of the limb that the foot is straight so that any forces within the joints are even. It is probably true that the majority of lower limb lamenesses are to a greater or lesser extent associated in some way with an incorrect hoof/pastern axis. Equally important is the balance between one side of the foot and the other.

The most common problem encountered is when the hoof/pastern axis is such that the line between the fetlock and the toe drops below a straight line. This is termed 'broken back'. The result is a long sloping foot due to insufficient trimming

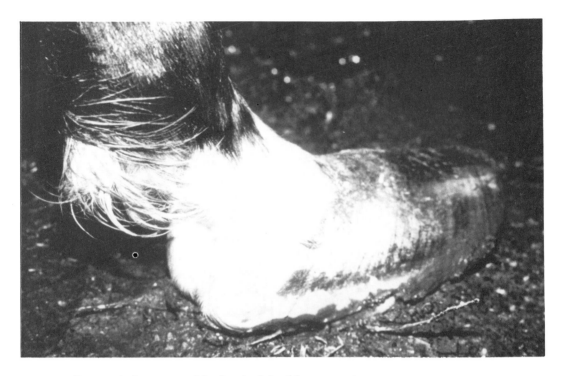

Fig 24   *Extremely long toe and broken back hoof/pastern axis.*

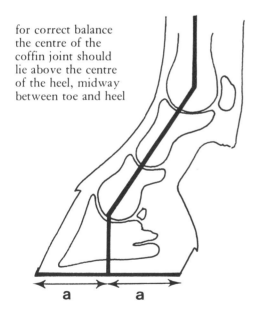

for correct balance
the centre of the
coffin joint should
lie above the centre
of the heel, midway
between toe and heel

a   a

Fig 25   *Weight displacement through the foot.*

of the toe from the anterior (front) surface of the hoof wall. Effectively the entire weight of the horse can be considered to pass through a point halfway between the point of the toe and the heels of the shoe. Where the toe is left too long the whole shoe is moved forward on the foot so that the centre point is transferred further forward, away from the actual weight of the horse which passes through the bony column (*see* Fig 24). The increase in the horizontal component of the forces that results inevitably puts severe strain on the supporting deep flexor tendon and associated structures at the back of the leg. The most important consequence of this phenomenon is that the horse begins to walk on his heels. The problem is further accentuated by the tendency to apply shoes that are too short at the heels so that the horse does not pull them off by over-reaching.

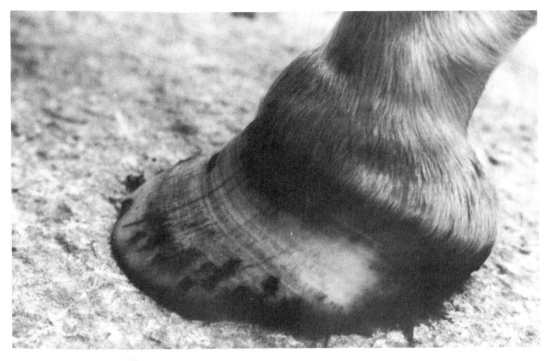

Fig 26 Horn tubules are bent by breakover of the toe when the hoof/pastern axis is broken back. Note the vertical stress fractures in the hoof wall.

Where the hoof/pastern axis is severely broken backward the horn tubes of the hoof wall are subjected to grossly abnormal pressures. This causes them to bend as the horse rolls the foot forward on to the toe as the toe leaves the ground, commonly called the 'breakover point'. At the same time the internal structures of the foot are being torn and internal bruising is taking place. The effect is the same as that in a person with a long nail that is forced backward. The subsequent tearing of the attachment of the nail is similar. If corrective action is not taken and the toe is allowed to grow even further then the subsequent tearing could result in traumatic laminitis.

A more common consequence of the horse walking on its heel, however, is that excessive pressure is applied to the structures at the heel. Under such pressure the heels start to collapse inwards. The internal structures of the heel are compressed to such an extent that the blood supply to the area, particularly to the navicular bone is severely compressed. This is an ideal breeding ground for navicular disease, the consequences of which will be discussed in detail in Chapter 7.

In contrast to the broken back hoof/pastern axis, when the line from fetlock to toe deviates above the normal, the axis is described as 'broken forward'. The effect of this conformation is that the hoof and fetlock become very upright. The result is that the stride becomes very short and the horse is uncomfortable to ride since the action is 'choppy' and stilted. The more upright bony column is

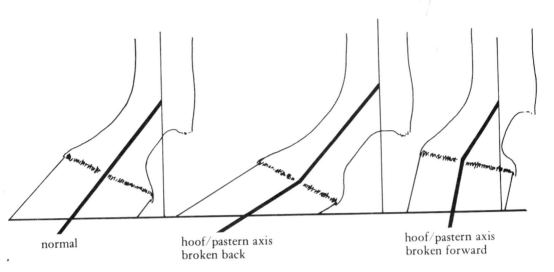

| normal | hoof/pastern axis broken back | hoof/pastern axis broken forward |

Fig 27 Variations in hoof/pastern axis.

subject to concussion and the fetlock is less well able to absorb the descending weight. Damage to the bone may arise in the form of ringbone or sidebone. The problem can be corrected by gradually trimming the heels but this cannot be done too quickly or severe strain will be applied to the supporting structures at the back of the leg.

Deviations of the Foot

The shape of the foot is affected by pressure. Any conformational abnormality will affect the pressures on the foot and lead to imbalance in the shape of the hoof.

'Toe in' conformation (pigeon toes) When a line drawn vertically through the centre of the hoof does not point directly in front of the horse, but is deviated inwards, the horse is said to have a 'toe in' conformation or to be 'pigeon-toed'. The horse will then stand with the toes close together. In this case the centre line from the shoulder through the knee is usually broken at the fetlock, although the knee

can be affected. The growth on the inside of the hoof is greater than on the outside, due to the excessive pressure on the outside wall where the majority of the horse's weight is taken. The wall on the inside also becomes wider and develops a wing. This wing must be removed when the foot is trimmed, to balance the feet and limb as much as possible. The flight pattern of the moving foot of a horse with this conformational defect is such that the foot swings outwards, or dishes.

'Toe out' conformation In contrast to the 'toe in' conformation, when the centre of the toe points away from the midline the condition is known as 'toe out'. Again, turning is usually from the fetlock, but less frequently it occurs from the knee. The wall of the hoof becomes upright on the inside with flaring on the outside wall. This again results from pressure due to abnormal weight distribution. Such conformation is likely to cause the two legs to interfere with each other, since during flight the affected leg

39

will swing inwards causing the foot to brush on the inside of the opposite leg. Serious bony damage may result.

Conformational Defects of the Hind Limb

The hind leg is designed in such a manner that it gains maximum propulsion from the large muscle mass of the hind quarters. The angulation of the stifle and hock allows the ability to flex and extend to be used to propel the horse forward. When viewed from the side the ideal horse should stand with the hocks slightly under the quarters. A line dropped perpendicularly from the buttocks should pass fractionally behind the point of the hock and end 3-4in behind the bulbs of the heels. A perpendicular dropped from the hip joint should fall between the toe and the heel of the foot. When this is the case the maximum weight falls through the centre of the foot. Viewed from the rear, the hock should be very slightly angulated so that the toe is turned fractionally towards the outside. Contrary to popular belief, the hocks should be slightly inclined together. This is clear if we consider the shape of the pelvis. The acetabulum into which the ball at the top of the femur fits is not parallel to the spine but is wider at the front. Therefore, to be comfortable, the front of the limb should point outwards.

Cow Hocks

Probably the most common fault in the conformation of the hind limbs is cow hocks. This defect describes the rotation of the limb so that the front of the limb points outward to a marked degree. Con-

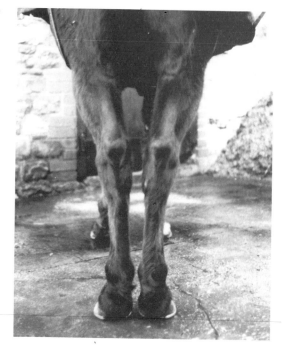

Fig 28   Cow hocks.

sequently the points of the hocks are very close together. The flight pattern of the limb is altered and moved in an arc towards the midline. As a result the horse tends to brush and nearly always causes some degree of interference with the opposite leg.

Sickle Hocks

When viewed from the side, the angle formed at the hock may become exaggerated. The cannon thus becomes more sloping as the foot comes to lie further forward than the perpendicular dropped from the point of the hip. At first glance this resembles a horse with laminitis that tucks its hind legs underneath the abdomen to support its weight. One effect of the abnormality is that excessive

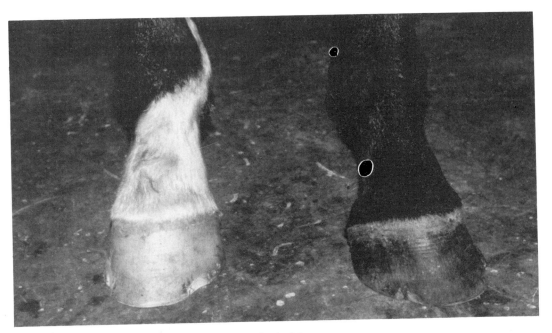

Fig 29   Turning out of the feet in the cow-hocked horse.

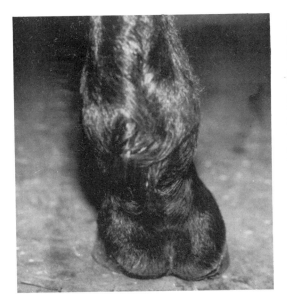

Fig 30   The fetlock must compensate for the rotation of the foot in the cow-hocked horse.

strain is placed on the posterior aspect of the hock joint possibly leading to the formation of curbs. Further strain is also placed on the hind quarters and the back. The toes grow longer and wear on the heels is excessive. In order to avoid further damage it is imperative to keep the toes short and provide adequate support behind the foot. This is done by shoeing with plenty of length behind the bulbs of the heels to support the legs, thus relieving the posterior aspect of the leg from as much pressure and strain as possible.

Straight Behind

In some horses the angle on the front of the hock is very large, in contrast to the horse with sickle hocks, so that the whole limb takes on a very upright appearance.

41

Where this happens the pasterns are usually short and upright and susceptible to concussive forces which may cause lameness. The abnormality may also affect the stifle joint. Excessive wear occurs at the toe, and where the problem is severe the trauma that results from the concussion leads to bruising.

Flight Pattern in Relation to Conformation

Before appreciating the flight pattern of the horse it is essential to understand the concepts of 'breakover' and 'footfall'. Breakover is the point at which the foot rolls on to the toe as it leaves the ground when the horse is in motion. When the foot is correctly balanced the point of breakover will be at the centre of the toe. The fact that all normally worn shoes indicate breakover at the toe has led some farriers to roll the toe of front shoes to help the action of the horse in breakover. Footfall is the point in time when the foot makes contact with the ground. Any abnormality in alignment of the limb will cause one part of the foot to land before another, and the footfall becomes uneven.

When considering flight pattern it is also important to look at the fetlock. Observing the normal limb from the side, the arc that the leg makes while in motion reaches its highest point when it passes the opposite limb. In this case the foot lands with the heel fractionally earlier than the toe, but essentially horizontal.

Broken Back Hoof/Pastern Axis

The long toe and low weak heels of the horse with a broken back hoof/pastern axis greatly affect the flight pattern of the foot. Since more weight is taken on the heels and the heels are lower than on the normal foot, the breakover, when the foot should leave the ground, is delayed. As a result the arc that is formed by the flight pattern of the leg is also delayed. The arc now reaches its highest point before it passes the opposite leg. The knee action is therefore reduced and the stride becomes longer and more sloping. More weight will be taken on the back of the leg during landing. The longer toe increases the effort required to achieve breakover and may cause the horse to stumble or trip over its feet. Considerable strains are placed on the internal structures of the foot, leading to strain on the deep digital flexor tendon, navicular disease, corn formation and occasionally traumatic laminitis.

Broken Forward Hoof/Pastern Axis

The short toe, high heels and upright pastern of the horse with broken forward hoof/pastern axis result in a flight pattern in which the arc reaches its peak after it has passed the opposite leg. The foot lands at an abnormally steep angle and the stride is shortened (see Fig 31). The flight pattern predisposes to problems related to concussion, namely ringbone, sidebone and to a lesser extent pedal ostitis.

When viewed from behind or in front, in the horse with perfect conformation the toe can be seen to be rolling over evenly. The knee bends and is brought forward in line with the fetlock. At a point just

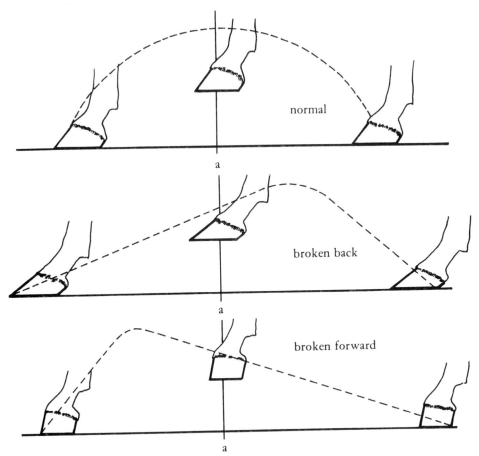

normal

broken back

broken forward

a = point at which the opposite (weight bearing) leg is passed

Fig 31   Variation of flight pattern with hoof/pastern axis.

before the foot is placed to the ground the knee, fetlock and point of the toe should be directly in line. The hoof must be placed absolutely horizontally on the ground.

'Toe in' Conformation

The horse with a 'toe in' conformation will breakover towards the outside of the foot. It does not move directly forwards but swings outwards in an arc. As the foot lands, the outside of the foot usually touches the ground slightly before the remainder of the foot. Such a flight pattern is unlikely to cause interference with the opposite leg. However, the uneven landing on the outside of the foot may predispose to the formation of sidebone on only the outer lateral cartilage of the pedal bone due to prolonged concussion. There will also be uneven concussion within the joints.

'Toe out' Conformation

In contrast to 'toe in' conformation, in 'toe out' conformation the foot breaks

43

over towards the inside. The toes are turned out so that the flight pattern is an arc inwards, which may cause interference with the opposite leg, the most common problem being brushing. Because the foot has swung inwards it will not land horizontally. The inside of the foot lands first. Again, the concussion can cause sidebone to form on one lateral cartilage, this time the inner (medial) cartilage.

It should be appreciated that these loose guidelines have over-simplified the situation to facilitate explanation. It is quite possible for a horse to have a toed-out conformation and wear the outside branch of the shoe, or a toed-in conformation and wear the inside branch, depending on whether the horse is base wide or base narrow. In horses that are base wide, the distance between the forefeet exceeds the distance between the shoulders whereas in base narrow horses the distance is less at the feet than at the shoulders.

Fig 32 'Toe-in' conformation.

Interference

Uneven trimming of the foot or natural imbalance of the foot lead to one leg interfering with the action of the opposite one.

Cutting or Brushing

When one foot strikes the opposite limb, usually in the area of the fetlock or foot, it is said to be brushing or cutting. This is usually confined to the hind limbs. Sometimes brushing causes only bruising but in more severe cases the skin is broken. The point of interference on the foot or shoe of the leg causing the interference depends on the conformation. The horse with cow hocks will brush with the heel quarter. When conformation is at fault the feet must be re-balanced to correct the defect.

The shoe to be fitted should be given careful consideration. A shoe that has been safed off, by taking off the sharp edge of the inside branch, and fitted tightly under the outline of the wall on the inside will prevent further brushing. In some cases where the foot is unbalanced, however, it may be necessary to fit the inside branch of the shoe outside the hoof wall. This gives the foot a balanced bearing surface from which the foot can breakover properly. This problem is most commonly managed by using a three-quarter shoe in which the inside branch is totally removed from the toe quarter to the heel. The rationale behind this approach is that by removing the offending part of the shoe the horse will cease brushing. In practice, however, the opposite occurs. Once the foot is deprived of its shoe over part of its surface the foot will automatically become unbalanced and the foot will tilt towards the inside. Even so, it is common practice to fit three-quarter shoes to race horses to prevent interference from occurring when the horse is racing at speed.

Brushing can also result from unlevel feet, risen clenches, shoes that have been left on too long and badly fitting shoes. The corrective action to be taken in these cases is self explanatory.

Speedy Cutting

Only the forelimbs are affected by speedy cutting which occurs at speed when the foot strikes the opposite leg just below the knee. The most susceptible horses are those with large flat feet and 'toe out' conformation. To avoid the problem the foot must be correctly balanced and a shoe applied which complements any conformational faults. It has been common practice to fit a shoe with the inside branch fitted under the foot from the toe to the heel quarter where it resumes the shape of the hoof wall. This should be avoided since it encourages the foot to break over on to the inside and unbalances the flight pattern even further.

Forging

Forging is frequently confused with over-reaching. When the toe of the shoe on the hind foot strikes the toe of the shoe of the front foot during motion a metallic clicking can be heard, known as forging. Sometimes forging can be habitual. The horse with a short back (short-coupled) and long legs is most susceptible to the condition. A further cause is poor riding in which the horse is unbalanced and not collected. The problem is helped to a limited extent by fitting the hind shoe with the toe well back under the wall. It is often helpful if the rider can be persuaded to seek advice regarding the schooling of the horse to a satisfactory standard. Young horses may undergo a phase in their development during which they forge, but the phase tends to be transitory. Occasionally injuries to the back lead to the horse becoming unbalanced with the result that they forge.

Dishing

The term 'dishing' refers to the process of swinging the front feet outwards while the horse is moving. The condition is often regarded as hereditary in nature since it is normally associated with unbalanced feet and 'toe in' conformation and the conformation may be hereditary. Dishing normally originates from the fetlock. Contrary to popular belief, there is no effective treatment for this abnormality apart from balancing the foot as much as possible. The belief that the problem can be corrected by applying weights to one side of the foot is a fallacy.

Over-reaching

Unlike forging, when the horse over-reaches he actually makes contact with the back of the leg. The interference is caused by over-extension of the hind limb. The toe of the hind foot strikes the

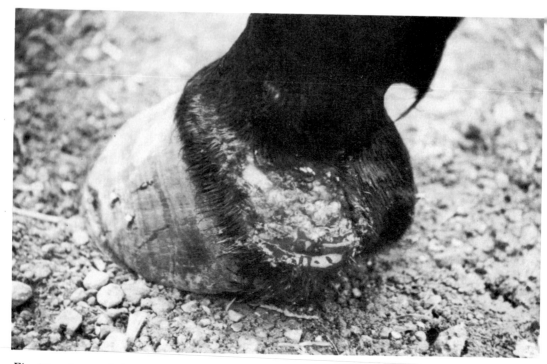

Fig 33 *A granulating wound of the outside heel caused by over-reaching.*

forelimb between the knee and the bulbs of the heels. Usually only the lower part of the limb is affected, particularly the bulbs of the heels. As over-reaching is affected by the action of both the fore and hind limbs special attention should be paid to the conformation. As with forging, the short-coupled and long-legged horse is more prone to injury. The feet should be balanced with particular regard to limb alignment. The toe of the hind shoe should be set well under the wall and this is normally sufficient to correct the over-reaching. By moving the shoe backwards slightly on the foot the chance of its interference with the foreleg is reduced. If this course of action is not sufficient to correct the problem the balance of the foot should be altered to increase the speed of breakover in the fore-limb. This is best achieved by fitting

a rolled-toe shoe and keeping the wall short at the toe, while leaving the heels of the shoe a little long.

Unfortunately the problem is associated with pulling the shoes off. The quality of a farrier should not be judged on the period of time that he is able to keep the shoes on a horse. Many factors contribute to the horse pulling off his shoes. First, the newly-shod horse rarely breaks the hoof wall when pulling the shoe off, which is often a cause for speculation. In fact, since the foot has just been trimmed it is short. The shoe is held on by only six or seven small clenches so that if it is pulled off at this time it will come away cleanly. If, on the other hand, the horse has six or seven weeks' growth on the foot it is more likely that the foot will break as the shoe is torn off. Also, by this time the shoe is no longer sitting on

Fig 34   Severe damage to the fetlock caused by over-reaching.

the wall, but has become embedded in the growing wall so that, although removal is much more difficult than immediately after shoeing, when it does occur, sideways movement is likely to cause the wall to tear with it.

It is a common fallacy that shoes just 'fall off'. All shoes that are lost are torn off by one means or another – with the exception of shoes that have been left on for so long that they fall off when the hoof becomes so long that the attachment becomes weakened. Ninety per cent of all shoes that are lost are front shoes which, if the farrier were to blame, would suggest that horses are properly shod behind but not in front!

All shoes that are torn off are found to be bent, however slightly, and often there are marks at the heel indicating that the horse has over-reached and pulled off the shoe. The horse that loses its shoe while being ridden can usually be recognised as having stumbled, or put in an extra stride whilst jumping, or been ridden through heavy going. In the case of the horse that loses its shoe while turned out, the freely running and bucking horse is not collected and is quite capable of pulling off a shoe at a moment of imbalance. The best way to avoid this unhappy event is not to fit a shoe with shorter heels. The fitting of longer heels allows the feet to breakover more quickly. The shorter the horse is shod the more retarded will be the action and breakover. If horses were kept and ridden in optimal conditions in which they were always collected and balanced, very few shoes would be lost. Shoes are not lost in wet muddy conditions because they are 'sucked off' but because the horse's action is retarded. Particularly in the jumping horse the foot cannot break over quickly enough to escape from the hind foot which follows. Consequently the horse over-reaches and pulls off a shoe. If this horse were to be shod with ten nails it would not make the slightest difference; the horse would still pull off the shoe.

3 Shoeing the Normal Foot and Associated Problems

The main object in shoeing the majority of horses is to increase the amount that they can be used. Horses are worked on abrasive surfaces and would suffer if not protected by the use of shoes. For this reason it is important when evaluating the horse's foot for shoeing to remember that the horse must be shod for comfort to obtain the maximum benefit. In the past the only criteria used to judge whether a horse was well shod were whether the shoe was of a length such that the heels fitted to the point of the heel and also that the shoe should resemble the size and shape of the foot. It is insufficiently frequently recognised that the horse should be shod with regard to its conformation and that each case should be treated on its own merits. The hunter-style shoe that has been adopted in Britain has undoubtedly been responsible for a large number of lamenesses associated with the feet and lower limbs.

Balancing and Trimming the Normal Foot

When viewed from the front the normal foot should be balanced. That is, a vertical line drawn through the centre of the bones should bisect the hoof. The inside

Fig 35 *The trimmed right foot compared with the untrimmed left foot. Both have been allowed to grow much too long.*

horizontal
component means
that increased force
is applied to the
inside of leg

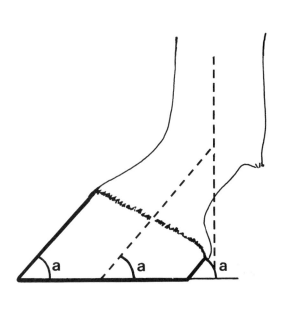

*Fig 36   Position of the centre of
gravity in relation to the limb.*

*Fig 37   Correct hoof angles at toe
and heel.*

wall is fractionally more upright than its counterpart on the outside. This will accommodate the slightly larger amount of weight being taken on the inside of the leg since the centre of gravity of the horse is inside, or medial to the whole leg. The angle between the front (anterior or dorsal) hoof wall and the ground surface should be exactly the same as the hoof/pastern axis and the angle of the heels (*see* Fig 37). When the foot is viewed from the ground surface it should be possible to divide it into two equal halves by drawing a line between the toe and the central cleft of the frog. The line should also pass through the point of the frog and the bulbs of the heels. The two halves should be mirror images.

The hoof must be correctly balanced to carry out its proper function. If the weight is unevenly displaced the growth and development of the foot will be affected. The information gathered during the essential period of observation of the moving and standing horse, with regard to hoof and limb alignment and conformation, will be used to determine the manner in which the horse should be shod to provide maximum long-term protection and comfort. The need to function properly is rendered the more important by the fact that the total weight of the horse and in some cases the rider also has to be taken and dissipated by the foot.

The foot is continually growing and should be trimmed every four to six weeks whether the horse is shod or unshod. If the horse is shod the shoes should be removed and the foot trimmed irrespective of the amount of wear on the shoe, at four- to six-weekly intervals. If the shoe is left longer than six weeks it will interfere with the growth of the foot and affect its natural function. Frequent trimming facilitates the early recognition of any abnormalities and corrective action can be taken to trim the foot to return it to normal. Over a period of time the new growth will alter the hoof/pastern axis, causing it to break back. Where the hoof/pastern axis is abnormal, or a conformational fault is present, trimming of the foot every three to four weeks may be desirable.

Once the foot has been trimmed to the required length and the correct hoof angles achieved, the next step is to check the balance from the front. This is the medial/lateral balance. It may be necessary when balancing the hoof to reduce the thickness of the hoof wall by removing the wing or long toe. This is done by rasping the outside of the hoof wall, contrary to commonly accepted procedure. For many years it has been customary to avoid touching the outer layer of hoof wall to avoid damaging the periople covering it. It was thought that by removing the periople the ability of the hoof to control its moisture content would be lost. However, there is probably no periople from half-way down the hoof wall to the ground surface. The re-establishment of a good hoof/pastern axis is far more important so that the foot can be balanced. In extreme cases it may be necessary to rasp the whole foot from the coronary band to the ground surface to correct the hoof/pastern axis and balance the foot. It should be understood, however, that if this drastic course of action is indicated it should be done over a period of time which may involve several shoeings. This will allow the horse to adapt to the new angles that the joints adopt, along with the changes in pressure exerted on the working surfaces of the joints. Whatever the circumstances, it is desirable to aim for the most natural shape and balance of the foot that is possible.

The frog is also being produced continually and should be trimmed when required. It is desirable to clean the sole and to remove all flakes of horny sole. If the horse has a tendency to develop large frogs then these, too, will need to be trimmed. Failure to do this may lead to over-expansion of the heels. As a result the frog is compressed excessively and it is impossible for the horse to bear weight on the wall of the unshod foot. After the foot has been trimmed the horse will be reluctant to place weight on the affected foot until the frog has been trimmed so that weight can be transferred on to the wall of the foot. Excessive frog is normally associated with flat feet.

Shoeing the Normal Foot

Forefeet

In the front feet the shoe at the toe should be a downward extension of the hoof wall. The standard shoe has one central clip which is situated at the centre of the toe. The heel quarters are fitted slightly wide of the outline of the hoof wall both inside (medially) and outside (laterally). This allows the foot to expand naturally. The heels of the shoe should extend slightly beyond the points of the heels, contrary to popular opinion which states

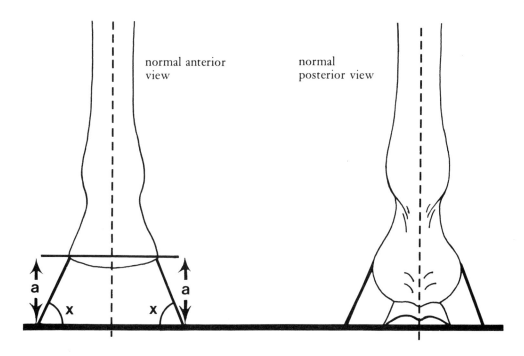

normal anterior
view

normal
posterior view

a

x x

a

Fig 38   Medial/lateral balance of the normal foot.

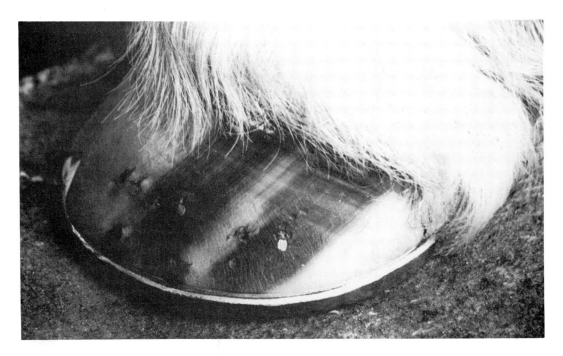

Fig 39   The well-shod forefoot.

that the two should be flush. By shoeing slightly long at the heels the balance of the foot and the comfort of the horse are immensely improved. Support is thus provided for the back of the foot and the leg, which gives a good stable foundation for the horse to work from. The shoe is nailed on to the foot using six or seven nails in the average foot, three on the inside and three or four on the outside. The small show pony requires only four or five nails whereas the large hunter requires six to eight nails. Although this is only a rough guide, in every case the minimum number of nails should be used to hold the shoe in place.

Hind Feet

The hind foot should be trimmed in accordance with conformation. As with the front foot, the main object is to obtain the most naturally balanced foot possible. The shoe is fitted to give the maximum protection and comfort. Because of the design and function of the hind leg it may become involved with problems of interference. The fact that the hind foot is usually fitted with two clips at the toe quarters means that the shoe can be fitted under the toe of the foot. It is closed in at the toe. Closing in is rounding off the ground surface of the shoe's outside edge to obliterate the fullering.

Fig 40   The well-shod hind foot. Note the length of the heel and the safing off of the toe to prevent over-reaching.

Fig 41   Ground surface view of the well-shod foot. Stud nails are placed on both sides of the shoe. Note that the shoe extends well back at the heels.

The hind shoe is fitted in this manner to ensure that, in the event of the horse over-reaching, the wall of the foot will glance off the back of the foreleg. If the shoe were fitted with a single clip injury would be far more likely. As with the forefoot the shoe can be fitted slightly wider than the contours of the hoof wall to allow for natural expansion of the foot. By fitting the heels long, support is provided to the back of the foot and leg.

Bar Shoes

Full Bar Shoe

The bar shoe is one of the most versatile surgical shoes in use today. It can be used to increase the bearing surface of the foot in order to distribute the weight over a larger area. This can be highly beneficial when treating such conditions as corns and pedal ostitis in those cases in which new bone on the ground surface of the pedal bone is pressurised by the descending body weight. A bar joins the heels of the shoe and renders it more rigid than a conventional one. As a result, pressure can be relieved from one part of the foot and transferred to another. During weight bearing the heels naturally expand independently of each other, separated by the frog. This can lead to such problems as shearing of the heels when one side is compressed more than the other. The movement on the inside and outside (medial and lateral) heels can be

53

reduced by fitting a full bar shoe. Such a shoe will also act as an external splint in cases in which the wing of the pedal bone is fractured. Where the hoof wall has been partly removed a full bar shoe should be applied to protect the underlying hoof structure and relieve pressure from the hoof wall, allowing new horn to grow. Finally, the shoe provides support to the bulbs of the heels where they have been damaged by severe over-reach.

Full bar shoes can thus be used in any event when the distribution of the horse's weight needs to be placed over a wider area, natural expansion retarded, or pressure relieved from part of the hoof wall.

Egg Bar Shoe

The egg bar shoe is a modification of the full bar shoe. Its main function is to distribute the weight of the horse over a

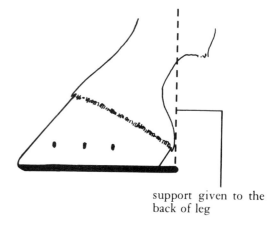

support given to the back of leg

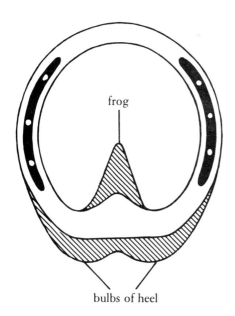

frog

bulbs of heel

Fig 42   The full bar shoe.

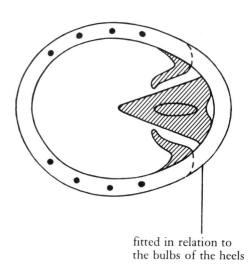

fitted in relation to the bulbs of the heels

Fig 43   The egg bar shoe.

Fig 44   The egg bar shoe supplies additional support to the heels.

larger area. The egg bar shoe differs from the full bar shoe in that the heels are not joined by a straight bar but by a semi-circular one that extends well behind the heels of the foot. This is a means of extending the heels of the shoe backwards while preventing material from catching on the extensions. The weight of the horse effectively passes through the centre of the shoe, but if the shoe has been extended backwards then its centre will also have been moved backwards. As a result the horizontal displacement of weight passing down the bony column is reduced. Compression of the underlying sensitive structures within the foot is also affected to such an extent that blood supply within the foot is enhanced by the fitting of an egg bar shoe. The shoe has a wide application in assisting the correc-tion of many conformational abnormali-ties.

The most common indication for its use is in the correction of the broken back hoof/pastern axis to support the low weak heels. The toe is usually rolled to assist breakover. The fitting to the out-line of the bulbs of the heels relieves tension from the posterior aspect of the leg by providing support.

In the past it was common practice to raise the heels to provide support for the leg. It is doubtful whether this form of treatment provides any support and in any event the egg bar shoe has the advantage of giving support while leav-ing the horse with a firm flat bearing surface. Many abnormal conditions of the foot, including navicular disease, sheared heels, injuries to the back of the

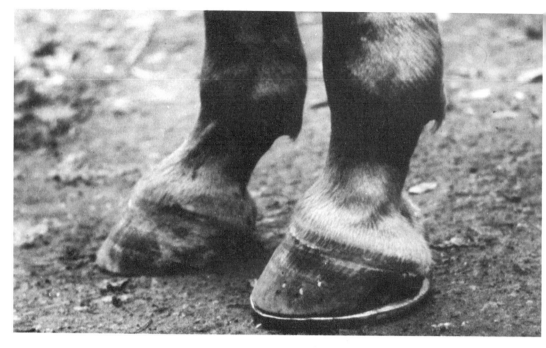

Fig 45 The egg bar shoe projects well behind the bulbs of the heels and is set in relation to these.

leg, corns, pedal ostitis, sidebone and laminitis, will all benefit from the use of this type of shoe although it will be appreciated that the long projection behind the foot will prevent the horse from being very active while the shoe is fitted.

Problems Associated with Shoeing

Flat Feet

The horse that does not have a natural concave shape to the ground surface of the sole is said to have flat feet. The vaulted shape adds to the strength of the sole in supporting some of the horse's weight. Flat feet can be a hereditary abnormality but the sole will become more flattened in horses that are turned

out on to wet or marshy ground. Horses that have laminitis also develop flattening of the sole due to pressure from rotation of the overlying pedal bone. Whatever the cause, flattening of the soles makes shoeing more difficult.

If a narrow-webbed shoe is used to concentrate all the load bearing on the wall of the foot the horse will become progressively more lame, since the shoe offers no protection to the sole. Weight is transferred on to the sole from the wall of the foot, and a shearing force is set up between the wall and the sole. In consequence, bruising may occur on the sole. Careful trimming of the foot is essential. The heels should not be trimmed and a wide-webbed shoe is applied. The shoe is seated out, or lowered slightly at the solar surface to relieve any pressure on the sole. Special attention should be paid when fitting the shoe to ensure that maximum

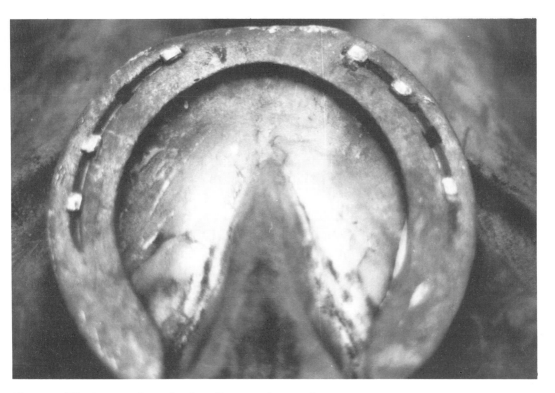

Fig 46   The broad web on the shoe disperses the weight over a wide area. This is particularly valuable when the horse has flat feet.

protection is given to the sole in this manner. The shoe should also be fitted long at the heels to relieve them of any undue strains or pressures. In some cases a full sole pad can be used to protect the whole of the sole, but this should only be used as a last resort.

Brittle Feet

Brittle feet are not the prerogative of one breed or horse, nor of a particular conformation. The tendency to have brittle feet can be inherited but the problem ultimately arises from the environmental influences. Most frequently they are seen in association with broken back hoof/pastern axis and are brought about by poor shoeing and inadequate trimming.

When nails are placed too low in the wall of the hoof in an effort to avoid nailing into sensitive tissue, the margin of the hoof is most liable to break off.

Stable management also has a bearing on the hoof structure. The effect of shavings or sawdust as a form of bedding is to dry the hoof, leaving it brittle. Vertical splits appear in the hoof wall in these cases. The cracks open when nails are driven into them. Such cracks are usually the result of a lack of moisture although nutritional deficiency may play a part. If the foot is not properly trimmed but allowed to flare at the ground surface, pressure will be created on the horn tubules, causing them to separate and the hoof to split. It is therefore essential to trim the foot and ensure that the angles of the hoof wall are correct. Brittle, shelly feet are also encouraged by the application of nails too low in the hoof wall, as has already been mentioned.

It is important that the appropriate shoes should be selected. A wide-webbed shoe will help to distribute weight over a larger area. The foot should be trimmed and all the loose horn removed from the front of the hoof wall. This may mean that it needs to be rasped from below the coronary band to the ground surface to obtain the correct hoof/pastern axis. The shoe should be fitted on with nails that can be placed to emerge above the weak shallow horn.

To avoid desiccation of the hoof the horse is probably best bedded on straw or peat. Feet that have dried should be washed with water as often as possible. It is fashionable to use biotin to help the treatment of this condition, but all too frequently this is not as an adjunct to corrective shoeing, but as an attempt to compensate for poor farriery.

Contracted Heels

When the horse's toe is too long, the hoof/pastern axis broken back and the weight is being transferred to the back of the foot, the heels become susceptible to contraction. It should be noted, however, that the heels may also become contracted when insufficient weight is placed on the foot to cause the heels to expand. Injury to the back of the leg or foot, or contraction of the tendons, are suitable reasons for this to happen. The result is that the heels turn inwards on the ground surface, towards the frog. Over a period of time,

probably extending over a year or more, the back of the foot reduces in size and interferes with the natural function and physical movements of the foot.

Low weak heels lead to pressure being taken on the heel area to such an extent that the growth rate of the heels is grossly reduced. The sequel to the reduction in growth rate is that the heels collapse inwards and contract under pressure. Besides correct trimming, the use of a wide-webbed shoe is essential, with the heels of the shoe fitted long to disperse the extra pressure. Once the pressure is relieved the hoof wall expands.

Injuries to the back of the leg or foot make the horse reluctant to bear weight on the heel area. If insufficient weight is taken the frog withers and tends to sink inwards. This condition is associated with horses that have a broken forward hoof/pastern axis. The short stumpy feet do not dissipate weight through the heel in the same manner that the correctly balanced foot would. The appropriate foot trimming of these cases involves reducing the height of the heels in an effort to re-establish movement to encourage expansion of the heels. Graduated shoes, in which the height of the shoe is reduced towards the heels, are beneficial.

Sheared Heels

Imbalance of the foot so that the bulbs of the heels are not of even height and the weight is not distributed evenly on the two sides of the wall is called sheared heels. The condition will be discussed in more detail in Chapter 7.

4 Adjuncts in Shoeing

Shoeing, like so many other forms of equine activity, follows trends and fashions. The development and use of heel wedges and hoof cushions have been the subjects of such fashions.

Wedges

There is little doubt that there is a place in farriery for heel wedges, and that they can be beneficially employed in certain selected cases. However, the indications for their use are far less than those in which they are actually used. They are valuable in resting the leg following injury to the deep flexor tendon. At one time they were extensively used in an endeavour to correct various conformational faults, and in show jumpers in an attempt to alter the horse's gait to allow it to jump higher.

It was, and sometimes still is, a common misconception that a long foot and broken back hoof/pastern axis with low, weak heels could be corrected by the application of wedges under the shoes at the heels. By raising the heels, so the argument runs, the whole leg would be raised and the height of the heel would be restored since the weight of the horse would be thrown on to the toe and

Fig 47   The wedge is trimmed to conform with the outer margin of the shoe.

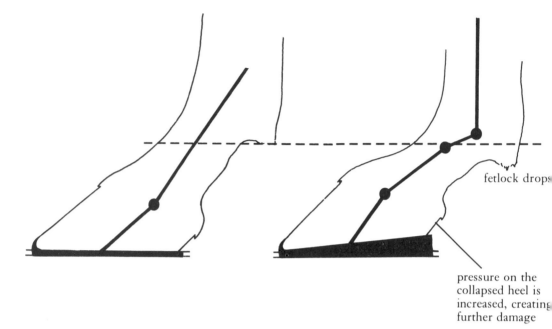

fetlock drops

pressure on the collapsed heel is increased, creating further damage

Fig 48 Effect of using wedges to correct broken back hoof/pastern axis.

reduced on the heel. In practice, the opposite effect is achieved. The back of the foot may be raised in the resting leg, but the full weight of the horse must still pass through the upright column of the leg during maximum weight bearing. By trying to insert a wedge under the heel, the pressure on the heel is actually increased. Compression of the heels leads to destruction of the wall and contraction of the heels (see Fig 48). The wall at the buttress of the foot leans forward due to excessive compression.

Wedges leave the horse with the impression that it is always walking downhill. The pressures applied to the working surfaces of the joints and to the bones and soft tissue structures are altered. In the normal horse the fetlock, supported by the superficial flexor tendon and the suspensory ligament and being used as a pulley by the deep digital

flexor tendon, acts as a shock absorber and in doing so may descend to touch the ground as the full weight of the galloping horse comes on to the leg. This is essential to reduce concussion passing through the joints, which might otherwise cause serious damage. The application of wedges raises the fetlock so that the descent to the ground is greater and over-extension of the joint correspondingly greater. Increased strain is therefore placed on the most vulnerable area. Support is much more effectively given to the back of the foot by the application of a shoe with long heels. In severe cases the ends of the heels of the shoe can be joined behind the foot to form an egg bar shoe. The centre of the shoe, and therefore the centre of weight bearing is moved back under the bony column of the leg and, at the same time, a level bearing surface is supplied for the horse to stand on.

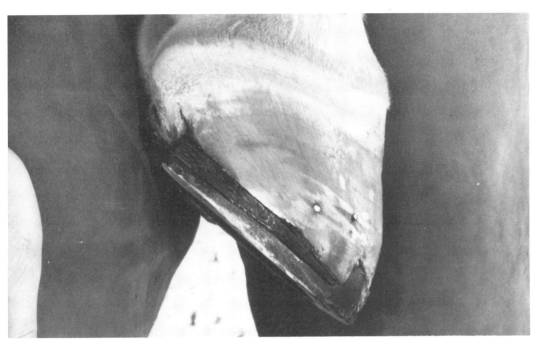

*Fig 49   Wedges can create enormous damage to the hoof wall in
the heel area, particularly when fitted with a shoe that is too
short at the heels.*

*Fig 50   Wedges create weak heels, breaking back at the
hoof/pastern axis and pressure on the internal structures
in the heel.*

Pads

Full sole pads which are fitted under the shoe cover the ground surface of the foot completely. They are usually made from plastic or leather. Horses with thin soles which are particularly in need of protection are suitable candidates for the use of sole pads, but soles damaged by penetration can also benefit from their use. The thin-soled horse has a sole that is unable to withstand compression from the ground contours so that the feet become sore. The application of sole pads may not always be beneficial to the horse since the exclusion of air from the sole may be detrimental to its condition. The sole becomes soft and moist but will dry out after a relatively short period of exposure to air. If the sole is naturally thin, however, this softening can only exaggerate the problem.

Care must be taken in selecting the correct type of shoe. A shoe is required that provides sufficient cover to the foot and support to the sole, maximising the comfort of the horse. Where the sole has been penetrated a full pad can be applied for short periods. Continued use of the horse in which pads have been fitted is likely to lead to the shoe being torn off and further damage to the foot. This happens because when the pad is applied the horse loses some of the sensitivity felt by the sole of the foot so that some fine co-ordination is lost. Also, because some shock is absorbed by the pad on impact, it is compressed slightly and the shoe is moved on the nail. In consequence, the shoe gradually loosens.

If the horse is carefully worked on rough surfaces over a period of time the sole will gradually harden and become acclimatised to the rougher conditions. If the sole is protected by pads this accommodation fails to take place.

Cushions

Hoof cushions take the form of thick pieces of plastic which fit beneath the shoe, with a thickened rim which fits along the inside edge of the shoe. Their function is to absorb concussion in bones that are susceptible to problems associated with concussion. These problems include sore shins, bruising to the sole, ringbone and sidebone.

The design is such that the concussion is absorbed through the plastic rim. Cushions rarely prove effective and usually lead to secondary problems such as bruising of the sole as a result of pressure exerted by the cushion. When they are fitted the edge on the solar surface is lowered to remove pressure on the sole. Once again a wide-webbed shoe should be applied. If the horse is still unhappy then a pad may be fitted beneath the shoe, sandwiched between the shoe and the foot and not covering the sole. The pad should resemble the shape of the shoe and be no wider than the width of the shoe.

Studs

When worked on smooth surfaces such as roads, horses often require the traction provided by studs to prevent slipping. The centre of the stud is made from tungsten carbide which is very hard and much harder-wearing than the shoe. The central tungsten core stands proud of the shoe to provide the grip. It is the common practice to fit only a single stud to the

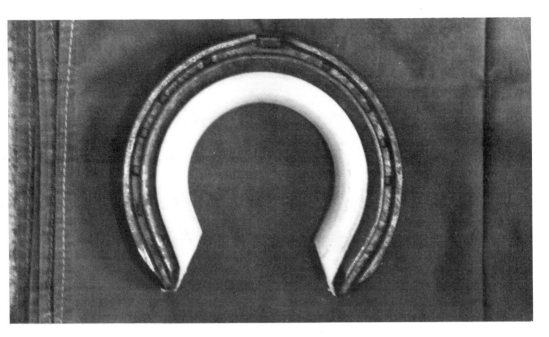

Fig 51   The cushion protects the sole and extends as a thin layer between shoe and hoof wall.

outside of the shoe at the heel. Studs are normally fitted as a matter of course to the horse being worked on the road since, although they are generally undesirable, they prevent the horse from coming down on its knees. Studs that are in common use fall into two categories: those that are small and fit flush to the shoe in the front and those that are larger with a mushroomed head, mainly used in the hind shoes. The fact that the small studs are level with the shoe means that they do not unbalance the foot when fitted. As the shoe wears, however, the pin stands proud of the shoe, increasing pressure on the outside of the foot. If studs are absolutely necessary, two of the smallest possible studs should be fitted, one in each heel. This balances the foot from side to side and prevents the drag on one side of the foot.

The larger stud with the mushroomed head should be avoided whenever poss-

ible. The normal practice is to fit them to the outside heel which renders the shoe and the foot uneven, the outside being up to a centimetre higher than the inside. The pressure that this places on the outside is so great that the wall collapses over a period of time and the result is clearly visible. The uneven pressure can cause unilateral sidebone. In addition the joints and working surfaces of the bones of the limb are affected by the uneven pressure placed upon them. This may predispose to ringbone and other arthritic changes within the joint. As the stud is the first thing to come into contact with the ground in the correctly balanced foot, it causes drag on the outside heel of the shoe so that as the horse walks the toe is rotated outwards. Consequently, as the horse moves, the foot screws outwards. The horse becomes cow hocked and brushing with the heel quarters is the final result.

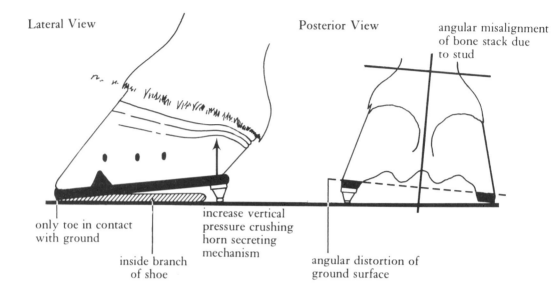

Lateral View Posterior View angular misalignment of bone stack due to stud

only toe in contact with ground

increase vertical pressure crushing horn secreting mechanism

inside branch of shoe

angular distortion of ground surface

Fig 52 *Effect on foot balance of using studs.*

Fig 53 *Stud nails project only a short distance below the ground surface of the shoe.*

An alternative to the use of studs is to utilise stud nails – ordinary nails with a tungsten carbide tip embedded into the head. They are effective in their action and do not alter the balance of the foot by raising the heel on one side. The horse is thus more comfortable and the foot has a level bearing surface. A further advantage is that the stud nails can be placed in whatever nail hole is required to be used.

Jumping studs are extensively used in show jumpers. These are screwed into holes that are drilled into the shoe and a thread tapped. Several different jumping studs exist, depending on the work for which the horse is intended and the conditions likely to be encountered. The large head of the jumping stud, it is argued, aids in the grip achieved by the horse and so helps in take-off and landing, and when turning within the ring. The increased friction, however, causes strain to the joints due to the shearing forces set up. It is recommended that the use of jumping studs be avoided. The studs should never be left in longer than necessary but should be removed as soon as the jumping has finished.

5   Specialised Shoeing

Long Distance Riding

Long distance riding is probably currently the fastest growing equine sport, with an emphasis on physical fitness. Rides vary in length up to 100 miles in a day and may extend over several days or more. Of all equine activities long distance riding is the most consistently gruelling. During this time the horse's feet are subjected to prolonged concussion irrespective of the terrain over which the ride takes place. Obviously the conditions are likely to change within a ride and some rides which involve a large amount of road work will produce more concussive damage than those on soft surfaces. Damage by sharp stones causing penetration of the sole is more likely on flinty downland as is the venue for the Goodwood Ride, for example, while bruising is more common where hard rough stones and rock are present on the Golden Horseshoe Ride, and many rides in the United States. Inevitably the horse suffers from fatigue sooner or later.

In shoeing the horse for long distance competition the emphasis is placed on safety and comfort. The shoes should fit according to limb conformation and should be comfortable and balanced. The prospect of riding large distances over rough ground has induced many people to use full sole pads under the shoes. The aim is to protect the sole from bruising or penetration by flints or sharp stones. Although pads will provide protection in the short term, in the long term they lead to softening of the sole and in many cases good farriery is preferable to their use.

The prolonged concussive effect on the feet can be dispersed by the use of a wide-webbed shoe. Sometimes a pad which is the same width as the shoe and fitted between the sole and the shoe can be helpful.

Several types of shoe could be used to advantage by long distance horses. Wide-webbed aluminium shoes are available which have mild steel inserts at the toes to extend the period of wear. These are very light and do not wear excessively provided that the terrain is not too rocky and hard. It is essential to keep the shoes as light as possible while providing the maximum cover to the wall and avoiding bruises and punctures. Where the ride is over rocky ground, 1.5×0.25in flat steel can be used. Although this material is very wide and therefore difficult to forge, when fitted, and the solar surface seated out, the shoes provide maximum cover to the foot and are reasonably light. However, their durability is limited and the horse would be capable of only a small amount of road work.

Show Jumping

Show jumping varies from the pony class at the local gymkhana to the Grand Prix class at an international show. All classes have the same ultimate aim, which is to jump as high and as fast as possible. It is important that the successful show jumper should be collected and well balanced. It has to be able to shorten or lengthen its stride at a moment's notice. It is required to turn and take off in confined spaces. The strains that occur on the joints, in consequence, are immense and many horses suffer from joint problems. Enormous power is necessary to work from the hind quarters to propel both the horse and rider over the fence without the advantage of momentum possessed by the steeplechaser. The landing is also steeper, the majority of the concussion being absorbed by the fetlock. The weight is then displaced on to the flexor tendons passing over the back of the fetlock, and the suspensory ligament.

The feet should be carefully trimmed to accommodate conformational faults and a shoe applied to provide maximum cover on the ground surface. Short toes and good support at the heels are the most important requirements.

It is common practice to use screw-in jumping studs in the shoes when competing. Jumping studs vary in length and type depending on the ground condition and are applied to improve the grip when jumping. The position in the shoe at which the stud is applied is a matter of preference although the heel is the most common site. Such studs are designed to be used only when the horse is jumping and should be removed immediately afterwards.

Driving

Whether a small trap or cart or a large wagon, the driving horse is required to pull loads. Since it usually works at relatively slow speeds the driving horse is unlikely to encounter interference prob-lems. The shoe is normally plain stamped and does not have any fullering or groove through the metal. This allows maximum wear. The toe of the hind shoe is thickened as this is the point at which maximum wear occurs. The horse must place the toe on the ground first in order to achieve the traction to pull the cart or carriage forward. The hind shoe is also fitted with a single toe clip to give added wear. In the larger driving horse it used to be customary to have calkins at the heels of the shoe to ensure that the horse did not slip. However, this is not recommended since the joints are jarred as the foot hits the ground and also the heels have a tendency to collapse.

The Race Horse

Like any other performance horse, the racehorse must have a reasonable conformation to enable it to do the job required of it with maximum efficiency. The usual principles with regard to the hoof/pastern axis should be monitored and the appropriate foot trimming should be undertaken. The shoeing of the racehorse is designed to achieve the maximum performance at speed. A light shoe is therefore applied. The stress placed on a horse during a race causes the horse to become fatigued at some point. At this time the horse becomes particularly susceptible to interference since tired muscles lose their ability to co-ordinate movement as finely as when fresh. The correctly fitted shoe is essential at this time. Besides being light, they support and protect the foot.

The going on which the horse races markedly affects the action. In very wet conditions the hind shoes may be

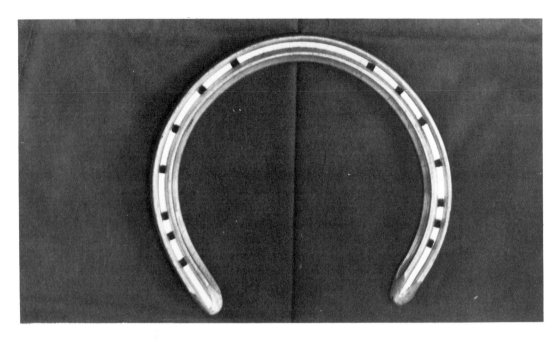

Fig 54   The aluminium racing plate.

removed to prevent the horse from striking into himself and causing injury to other limbs. The front shoes are fitted in relation to the shape of the foot. The hind feet are fitted with a three-quarter shoe. This is a shoe that has the inside branch removed from the heel quarter. As a result, brushing or interference with the opposite leg by the inside branch of the shoe is prevented. It is normal practice to remove the light aluminium shoes after racing and to replace them with working steel shoes.

National Hunt horses are not required to race at the same speed as the flat horse although the distance is usually greater and there are a number of fences to negotiate. Consequently the National Hunt horse often races in its light steel plates. Normal rules apply concerning the hoof/pastern axis. The front shoes are lighter than the normal working shoes and again a three-quarter shoe may be fitted to the hind feet. The outside heel

may have a calkin fitted to provide more grip whilst jumping, even though Jockey Club rules forbid the protrusion of nails by more than a sixteenth of an inch proud of the surface of the shoe.

The Show Pony

Show pony classes are divided from small, leading rein ponies to larger, riding pony classes. Whatever the class, any successful show pony must have a good conformation enabling it to move freely and correctly. The flight pattern of the feet of the show pony is that of a 'daisy cutter'. This describes the pony's ability to perform exaggerated movements from the shoulder. The leg moves straight with very little knee action. When the leg extends forward the toe of the foot points forward. The pony should move gracefully and freely and the action should be flowing and natural.

It is a common misconception that the required action can be brought about by altering the shoeing. The action must be natural and can only be enhanced by correct shoeing. The ability to move straight and correctly must be present in the pony from birth. Certain breeds of pony have an inherent ability to move better than others.

To allow the pony to move as freely as possible it is desirable to shoe with very light steel plates or aluminium shoes. Many good quality ponies are ruined by the use of shoes that are too heavy. The feet should be trimmed level from front to back and the heels should not be lowered to help the pony to 'daisy cut'. Unlevel trimming is a common practice among many farriers who are under duress from the owner. Although unlevel trimming will alter the flight pattern to achieve the desired action it is not good practice and should be avoided. If it is necessary to improve the action by shoeing, the light steel shoe should be replaced by an aluminium shoe just before the show – the action will automatically lighten with the lighter shoe. To gain the optimal performance it is best to shoe the hind feet with light steel plates while shoeing the forefeet with aluminium. Since the front limb is lighter than the hind the movement will be exaggerated. If aluminium shoes are used the heels can be tapered slightly, leaving the toe of the shoe a little heavier. In consequence the toe will be pointed forward during motion. The first consideration is, however, that the pony be fitted with shoes that give the foot protection and cover and do not deprive it of metal at the heels.

The Welsh Cob

Of all the showing classes, that for Section D Welsh Cob stallions is likely to be among the most popular with spectators. The criteria used in judging Welsh Cobs are similar to those used for other showing classes, with emphasis on good conformation and well-proportioned limbs. Unfortunately, the ability to move straight does not appear to be a sufficiently important prerequisite. The Section D Cob is required to have a very high knee action so that the limb is extended forward with force.

One of the gait abnormalities most commonly associated with the Welsh Cob is dishing with the front feet. This may result from excessively rapid growth of the young horse. In order to be successful in the show ring horses are required to be overweight, so the young horse is necessarily over-fed and the rate of growth is forced. The excessive weight passing through the growth plates of the long bones while they are still active, usually applying uneven pressure, results in a local inflammatory response and enlargement of the joints. This is most noticeable at the knees, fetlocks and hocks. The relative proportions of the minerals calcium and phosphorus in the diet also play an important role.

Furthermore, the showing of these horses from an early age renders it necessary that shoeing be started very early. Many Welsh Cob judges would not contemplate placing an unshod horse, irrespective of its conformation, anywhere other than at the bottom of the line. In some cases the application of shoes to the young horse may be detrimental, impeding natural horn development.

To achieve the necessary exaggerated action many horses are shod using heavy sections of metal. Usually the shoes are weighted at the toe to produce the high knee action and the short stride. The guidelines contained in the rule book of The Welsh Pony and Cob Society restrict the total weight of the shoes to be used on the horse, but these rules are frequently abused. This is in spite of the fact that the recommended weights are far in excess of those which should normally be carried by a horse of that age.

Any weight on the end of a limb acts as a pendulum and follows the laws of centrifugal force. Any deviation or abnormality of the limb will undoubtedly be exaggerated by the application of a heavy shoe and dishing, for example, will become far more obvious. To ensure correct alignment of the limb the horse should be allowed to develop naturally without carrying too much body weight. If shoeing at an early age is unavoidable then a light section of iron should be used. In every case the conformation and development of the limbs must be closely monitored and corrective trimming undertaken where necessary. The sooner that corrective action is undertaken, the more successful it is likely to be.

6 The Diagnosis of Lameness

Lameness is not a condition of the horse but a symptom of a condition and before successful treatment can begin the exact nature of that condition must be identified.

The shoulder of the horse or pony is extraordinarily frequently implicated by its owner as the cause of lameness. This is the more remarkable since shoulder lameness is comparatively rare. Although it is widely and correctly believed that the cause of forelimb lameness arises usually in the foot, it is a common misconception that any such lameness will be clearly visible to the naked eye, often without even removing the shoe. Moreover, that if the cause of lameness cannot be seen in the foot, the site of lameness must be in the shoulder. The logic behind this line of argument is difficult to follow and appears to have little or no foundation. Apart from anything else, it precludes all lameness arising from the pastern, fetlock, knee and elbow, and all structures between. In short, shoulder lameness has become a 'dustbin diagnosis' for any forelimb lameness, the cause of which is not immediately obvious.

Pinpointing first the site and then the cause of lameness requires a methodical and meticulous approach which may, in difficult cases, require two or three sessions each involving several hours. It is usually possible to establish the site, if not the actual cause, of lameness, but even then a proportion of causes remains a mystery. The problem is further compli-cated when more than one leg is involved as, for example, in the pony with laminitis, in which all four feet may be affected, or where the pain is at several sites in the same leg.

Initial Examination

Much research has recently been directed towards developing techniques employing modern technology to aid in the diagnosis of the cause of lameness, but it should be remembered that in the vast majority of cases, the cause of the lameness can be identified by careful consideration of the circumstances surrounding it and by a thorough examination of the horse. This examination needs to be both at a distance, with the horse first stationary and then moving, and in close detail using nothing more than a hoof knife and a pair of hoof testers to apply pressure to small areas of the hoof wall, sole, frog and bulbs of the heels. Close attention must be given to every detail of this part of the examination. The more sophisticated techniques should be used merely to confirm the suggestion of a problem.

The diagnosis of lameness is similar to the detective work involved in solving a crime. Evidence must be present before we can reach a reliable conclusion, although the evidence may, on occasion, be purely circumstantial. In establishing the cause of lameness a completely open mind must be maintained until definite

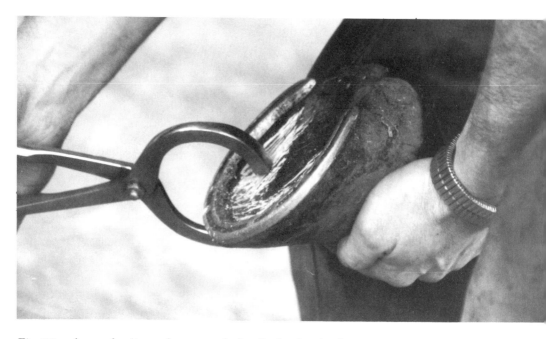

Fig 55   Areas of pain can be accurately localised using hoof testers.

evidence points the diagnostician in a particular direction. Nevertheless, the age and type of the horse should be borne in mind, together with the work which it has been undertaking in both the immediate and long-term past, since these factors will influence the likelihood of a particular condition being present. Infective joint disease, for example, is far more common in foals than in adult horses, while non-infective joint disease of the shoulder, elbow or stifle, or several joints at once, is more frequent in the young, maturing heavy horse. Chip fractures of the knee are most common in the racing thoroughbred, whereas laminitis is very rare in this group of animals. Specific conditions cannot be completely eliminated, however, on the basis of chance. Fractures of the second phalanx or short pastern bone are common in horses in the United States where horses are turned sharply in barrel racing and cutting. In Britain such fractures are rare but they do occur occasionally.

The speed of onset of the condition and the activity that was being undertaken at the time of onset should also be considered. The horse that develops an acute lameness and pulls up during a gallop is unlikely to have lameness arising from infection in the foot, whereas lameness is unlikely to arise from a fracture when the horse has been standing quietly in its box, unless it has recently become cast. Lameness which has gradually increased in severity over several days suggests development of an abscess and the build-up of pus. A similar cause may, however, result in a horse that was sound in the morning being unable to put its foot to the ground by evening, thus resembling a horse with a broken bone in the leg. Where slowly increasing lameness occurs several days after shoeing, or after a short period of acute lameness while out at

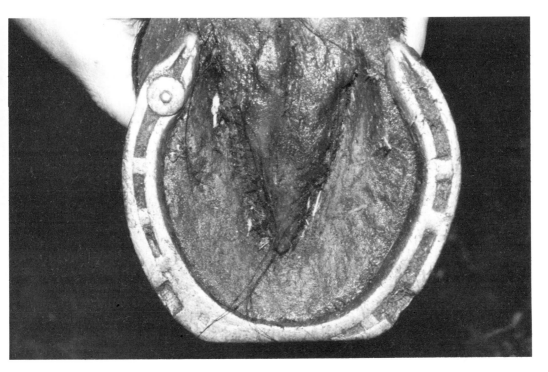

Fig 56   Improper flexion of joints over a prolonged period causes dragging of the toe which can quickly be identified in the wearing of the shoe.

exercise, this adds weight to the probability of infection in the foot. In the former case a nail placed too close to the live tissue of the foot may introduce an infection (so-called 'nail bind'), in the latter, infection is introduced when the horse treads on something sharp which penetrates the sole or frog. Usually the short period of acute lameness as the injury is inflicted rapidly resolves and is followed by a day or two of soundness before lameness re-occurs with steadily increasing severity.

Observation of the horse while standing at rest in his box or field is important. First, look at the horse's general attitude and demeanour and try to establish whether the cause of lameness is confined to the locomotor system or whether it is part of a generalised illness, which may affect several systems. Laminitis and tetanus fall into this latter category.

Next, assess what proportion of weight is applied to each leg, and the posture that is adopted. The horse with damage to the flexor tendons behind the cannon bone may lift the heel and take the weight on the toe to relieve tension on the tendons. The pony with laminitis will push both its forefeet out in front while tucking the hind feet underneath itself in order to take its weight. Navicular disease may cause the horse to 'point' one toe while at rest or to alternatively point one toe and then the other. These are not hard and fast rules but they are useful indicators. Other conditions cause similar signs and the conditions mentioned may not produce the signs described. For example, laminitis is usually more severe in the forefeet, but in cases where the hind feet are more seriously affected these may be pushed out behind the horse and a 'rocking horse' stance adopted, together with a shuffling gait not unlike that of the horse with tetanus.

At the initial examination gross abnormalities will be immediately obvious – a distortion of the limb resulting from a fracture, a large swelling of a joint or tendon, or a skin wound. More often, however, nothing will be obvious and it may not be clear that the animal is lame or which leg or legs are affected. To fully appreciate the lameness it is necessary first to walk the animal in hand and then to trot it. Since the trot is a simple two-time gait in which the lame leg is supported by only the diagonally opposite leg during weight-bearing, lameness is usually most apparent at this time and can often be evaluated within three strides. Moving in circles will provide more information than on the straight since weight is applied more to the inside limb than to that on the outside, and more to the outside of the inner limb and the inside of the outer limb. Consequently, although lameness is usually exacerbated when the painful limb is on the inside, where the site of pain is on the inside of the leg, lameness may be most obvious when the painful leg is on the outside of the circle.

The study of gait over different surfaces can also be valuable. Where pain arises from the foot, rough stony surfaces may render the condition much worse, whereas soft tissue injuries such as tendon damage will be more obvious on soft ground. Observing the degree of movement of each part of the limb and the manner in which the horse places its foot to the ground will also be helpful. Where present, the use of a hill to shift the horse's weight on to its hind quarters while going uphill, or on to the forequarters while going downhill can be helpful in exaggerating a lameness. Certain gait abnormalities can be emphasised by asking the horse to reverse, as is the case with horses that have stringhalt or are shiverers, particularly uphill. A sandpit helps to exaggerate soft tissue lameness during lungeing as greater strain is placed on muscles, tendons and ligaments.

Analysis of the horse's gait in slow motion by filming the horse's action and slowing the film has limited application since ordinary video filming is not sufficiently accurate to be of value and high speed cinematography is beyond the financial reach of most diagnosticians of the lame horse.

By holding the limb for half to one minute with one joint in the flexed position, pain arising from that joint may be increased so that when the horse is trotted away lameness becomes more marked. Each joint can be flexed in turn but it may be difficult to flex some without simultaneously flexing others. This is particularly true in the hind leg so that the so-called spavin test is not specific to the horse with a spavin or even with a hock problem. Indeed, the most marked response to a spavin test comes from a horse with a stifle problem. Forced flexion tests need to be interpreted with care in all cases since lameness can be created by excessive flexion of a normal joint. If this is the cause of lameness, however, the horse will become sound in two or three strides, whereas it will persist if a pathological process is present in the joint.

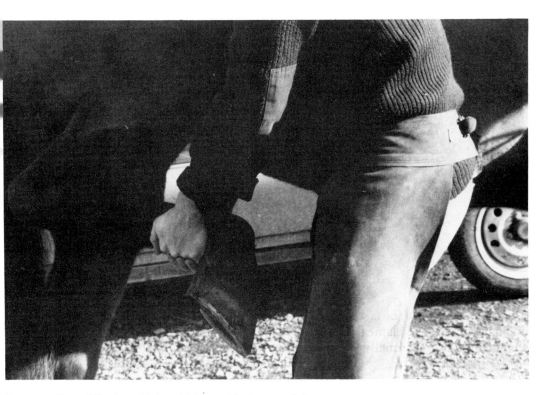

Fig 57   Forced flexion of injured joints will often result in increased lameness when the horse is trotted away.

Detailed Examination

The next phase of the examination is to look closely at each part of the affected leg or legs. Since most frequently the cause of lameness is in the foot it is logical to start at the foot and to move up the leg, looking for areas of heat, swelling, pain when pressure is applied or resistance to movement. The shape of the foot may yield important clues. Where the feet are not a matching pair it is likely that lameness arises from the foot, particularly where the horse is lame on the leg with the smaller foot, since a boxy foot indicates a prolonged period during which full pressure has not been applied to the foot. A boxy upright foot therefore indicates a chronic lameness,

probably with a duration in excess of a year.

The Hoof Wall

The condition of the hoof wall can also offer valuable information. Hooves that are badly cracked or broken around the ground surface are susceptible to infection which may become established through the cracks and run under the hoof wall. If the crack extends up the hoof as far as the coronary band or is deep enough to involve deeper sensitive laminae then lameness may result without infection needing to be present.

Rings running parallel to the coronary band around the hoof merely indicate a change in the rate of growth of the hoof.

Although frequently called 'laminitic rings' they are not necessarily indicative of chronic laminitis. The confusion arises since laminitis in fat ponies often follows a change in diet that is reflected in a change in growth rate of the hoof wall. Furthermore rings do arise in the hoof wall of horses with laminitis due to changes in growth rate brought about by altered pressure on the coronary band – in this case the rings are not parallel but diverge towards the heels.

When viewed from the side, the profile of the front of the hoof wall is assumed to be straight, but this may not be so. A change in the growth rate resulting from a change in the pressure reflected from the bearing surface to the coronary band may cause quite a marked angulation in the hoof wall.

If the toe is long during walking it will be levered away from the foot. The ensuing separation of the wall from the sole produces a crack up which infection can travel. Where the toe has been allowed to become too long the heels are often unsupported. This is particularly common when the shoes have been left on too long or the shoe has not been extended far enough backward when it was applied. The result is that the heels collapse inwards, applying pressure on the underlying structures. In the short term the pressure applied by the ends of the shoes produces local bruising, more commonly known as corns, while in the long term the navicular bone may have its blood supply restricted which leads in turn to destruction of the navicular bone and the start of navicular disease.

Swelling

The site of a swelling in the leg does not necessarily indicate the site of injury. Fluids will follow the line of least resistance, generally up the leg. Because it is unable to accumulate beyond a certain level inside the foot, for example, due to the inability of the hoof to expand, it will break out after several days either through the skin at the coronet immediately above the site of entry into the sole, or it will spread along the connective tissue around the major structures of the leg. As a result, the pastern will swell, then the fetlock, then particularly around the flexor tendons behind the cannon and up to the knee, leaving the casual observer with the impression of damage to the tendons themselves. Differentiation of these two conditions is vital since treatment for the wrong condition may result in considerably more damage being done.

Heat in the feet should be carefully evaluated, comparing one foot with the others. The hooves will all become warmer when the horse moves around on them and one hoof may become quite warm if the horse is standing with sunlight falling on to that foot. Heat in the foot is not necessarily synonymous with infection in the foot although this is often the case. Any disease process going on within the foot may cause heat production. Conversely, absence of heat from the foot does not exclude the foot as the site of injury.

All too often the site of lameness is still not obvious after these initial examinations. However, a decision has to be made regarding whether the foot is responsible for lameness, especially if the horse is shod, since the shoe will need to be removed and the whole area examined closely for a small black mark denoting a penetrating tract. By carefully exploring such tracts and judiciously applying pressure to various parts of the foot, the answer can often be found.

Regional Anaesthesia

One slow but effective method of pinpointing the site of lameness is to progressively anaesthetise the nerves running down the leg so that the area supplied by the blocked nerve loses its pain sensation. By starting at the level of the pastern to anaesthetise the heels, and progressing up the leg until the horse becomes sound, the area of pain can be fairly accurately located. Further accuracy can be achieved, but much more slowly, by anaesthetising each side of the leg separately. Some structures become anaesthetised more quickly than others so that although sensation in some structures may be lost within five minutes, others may take longer and it is necessary to wait at least twenty minutes before definitely concluding that the lameness has not been eliminated.

Where the lameness is not the result of pain but is mechanical as, for example, when the leg cannot be extended properly due to a relative contraction of the tendons or ligaments behind the leg, or when nerve paralysis prevents messages being

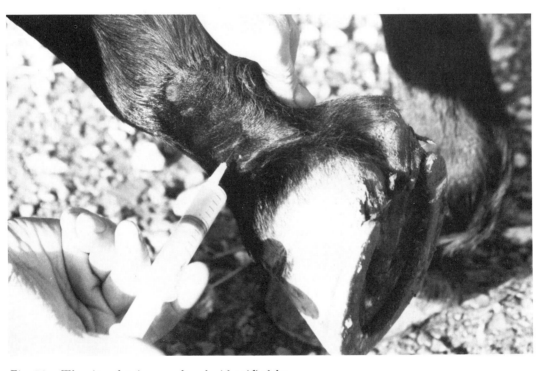

Fig 58   The site of pain can often be identified by anaesthetising the nerve supply to a specific area.

sent to the appropriate muscles to move the limbs, then lameness may not be improved at all, or at best be slightly improved. Furthermore, if the horse is expecting movement to be painful it may be some time before it realises that the pain has been eliminated. Sometimes when lameness is blocked out on one leg the horse will become lame on another leg. This phenomenon is not uncommon and usually occurs when lameness in both legs is from the same cause, as will be the case in laminitis, navicular disease or bone spavin. It is important to verify that the cause of lameness in each leg is the same.

The placement of local anaesthetic within a joint may also be helpful but it should be remembered that often, where a joint is injured, the surrounding soft tissue structures are also affected and remain painful when local anaesthetic is introduced. Conversely, local anaesthetic may affect a nearby area, eliminating lameness where the joint itself is not actually involved.

Once an area has been anaesthetised, the effect will take several hours to completely wear off. To avoid confusion it is preferable to perform only a few blocks at a time and, clearly, where a joint is implicated by regional block, local anaesthesia of the joint itself cannot be carried out on the same day.

Before the technique can be used, the horse has to be sufficiently lame that we can be sure that an improvement has occurred when the appropriate area has been blocked. Paradoxically, it is often the horse that is only slightly lame or that is inconsistently lame that is the most difficult to evaluate. If the horse is known to sometimes go sound after a period of exercise or to have a lameness which shifts from one leg to another, then we do not know with any degree of certainty whether such changes have occurred as a result of the local anaesthesia or whether they would have happened anyway.

X-Radiography

Where the site of lameness has been located and the cause is thought to involve the bony skeleton, X-radiography is often helpful to try to demonstrate damage. Often, however, exactly the correct angle or position is required to demonstrate a crack or presence of new bone that is forming. Several slightly differing positions may be required to demonstrate a problem. Hair-line fractures may not show at the time that they occur but, when re-examined radiographically ten days later, they may become obvious.

For these reasons radiography can only be used to verify or to eliminate a diagnosis that has already been tentatively made. It is easy to see how problems can arise when radiographs are taken as part of a routine examination for the purchase of a horse. It is of no use to X-ray a foot, for example, and, seeing nothing, assume that there is no problem there. Radiography will not demonstrate many of the problems which may be present in soft tissue. A splinter of wood tracking along the underside of the hoof wall would not be visible. There may even be bony damage which has not been demonstrated.

Different bones and even different parts of the same bone require different intensities of X-rays to produce the correct exposure to indicate an abnormality. The correct intensity to show the margin at the toe of the pedal bone would not penetrate the same bone at the coffin joint, so that a crack here would easily be missed at that exposure. Also the beam of X-rays must be pointed in the correct direction. A bone spavin can easily be missed by taking radiographs of the hock from front to back and from one side to the other, when the abnormality can often be demonstrated only by directing the beam obliquely across the joint in a plane parallel with its surface. We can see, therefore, that the expected findings must be known before the search begins.

Specialised Techniques

Thermography

If the site of lameness has still not been identified, further, more specialised techniques may be employed. Thermography involves the use of a heat sensor to detect slight variations in body temperature. Working on the principle that an area of inflammation will result in a local increase in heat production, thermography measures this heat and displays it as a contour map on a screen. By comparing the map with one produced by the opposite limb local areas of heat and therefore, possibly, injury can be located. Theoretically this could be useful in the early diagnosis of tendon injuries, but in practice the tendon probably undergoes degenerative rather than inflammatory changes prior to injury and no heat is produced.

Scintigraphy

Perhaps more useful but more complicated is the use of scintigraphy. Far from being a dead, inert substance, bone is active, changing and re-shaping itself constantly. When damaged, bone becomes more active during the repair process. If a substance which is preferentially absorbed by bone (methylene diphosphonate) is labelled with a mildly radioactive tracer (technetium 99) and injected into a vein, it can be measured several hours later using a scintillation counter. Again, by comparing the opposite limb, high levels can be reliably detected in areas of bone damage. When followed by radiography this can be a highly efficient diagnostic tool in cases of bone damage. In spite of common and understandable fears that the radiation produced may be dangerous both to the horse and the handler, the low intensity of radiation used and the rapid rate at which it is removed from the body mean that the technique carries no greater risk to health than does X-radiography.

Ultrasound Scanning

Damage to ligaments and tendons, most commonly the flexor tendons and suspensory ligament running down the back of the cannon bone, can be examined using an ultrasound scanner. This sends a very high frequency sound wave through the structure before being bounced back to a detector, following the same rules as light reflecting off a mirror. Degree of reflection depends on the density and the uniformity of the structure so that areas of blood accumulation and disruption of normal structure can be visualised. Consequently a more accurate assessment can be made of the period of time likely to be required for a full recovery.

Arthroscopy

The evaluation of joint disease has been facilitated by the recent increase in use of the technique of arthroscopy. Damage within a joint can be demonstrated by radiography only when the surfaces have become sufficiently affected to cause damage to the underlying bone, or new bone has begun to form around the diseased joint. In either case the damage has progressed by that stage and the prospect of full recovery is reduced. Where the joint is large enough an arthroscope can be introduced through a puncture into the joint so that the joint surfaces and surrounding soft tissue structures can be seen, and an accurate evaluation can be made.

Faradism

Where the lameness results from injury to muscle, faradism can be used to detect such an injury. Applying a small electric current across an individual muscle or group of muscles, can cause them to contract independently. When this is done to damaged muscle the pain produced will cause the horse to produce an exaggerated response.

Analgesics

Finally we must decide whether lameness is the result of *inability* to move correctly (mechanical lameness) or of pain during movement. Where the seat of that pain is high in the limb or has persisted for some time so that the horse expects pain when it moves, local nerve blocking is inappropriate. In these cases a short course of pain reducing drugs (analgesics), usually given by mouth, can be informative.

Hind Limb Lameness

It is fortunate that hind limb lameness is less common than lameness in the forelimb. Hind limb lamenesses are more difficult to see, or to feel when the horse is being ridden. Studies have demonstrated that it is very difficult, if not impossible, to diagnose the site of lameness merely by looking at the way in which the horse moves. Although lameness in the hind limb still arises most commonly from a problem in the foot, more problems arise from higher up the leg. Of the sites higher in the leg, the hock is most frequently affected. Furthermore, hock lameness often affects both hocks, one more severely than the other. Because the anatomy of the stay apparatus of the hind leg ensures that most of the joints flex to the same degree when one is flexed, a flexion test of the hock (the so-called 'spavin test') indicates only that there is pain in one of these joints.

The hind legs carry approximately thirty per cent less of the horse's weight than do the forelegs. Consequently, the conditions that result from the horse's weight being driven through an upright column (flexor tendon damage, ringbone and navicular disease, for example) are less important. In the hind legs, which are more important for propelling the horse forward, problems arise more frequently from the driving force, namely the muscle mass at the top of the leg, and from frequent flexion of the complex joints. When such lameness is insidious in onset and progressive over a long period of time there is often little or no inflammatory change visible from the outside and the only feature is incomplete flexion of all the joints of the leg causing dragging of the toes during movement. Some horses drag their toes through laziness but these can be differentiated from toe-dragging due to pain during flexion of joints by flexion tests and the use of analgesics for a short period.

Although lameness resulting from injury to the back is much less common than is generally believed, this will frequently cause lameness in both hind legs. This further confuses identification of the source of hind limb pain.

Where the muscle of the hind quarters does not function adequately the horse may show overt lameness or the inability to use the legs properly. Not infrequently this results from an imbalance of minerals in the functioning muscle cells so that muscle contractions are weaker than normal. The estimation of the levels of these minerals, principally calcium, sodium and chloride, in samples of blood and urine taken simultaneously will highlight such a problem so that appropriate corrective action can be taken. Any response to treatment will occur rapidly so that the affected horse is moving normally within ten days. Blood samples can also be used to identify the degree of acute muscle damage which may be present, since damaged muscle cells release enzymes (organic catalysts) into the blood and these can be biochemically detected. The peak enzyme levels present have a direct correlation with the degree of damage that has occurred.

When used in the hind leg, diagnostic techniques commonly used in the diagnosis of forelimb lameness – those of nerve-blocking sequentially up the leg and X-ray radiography – are neither as easily performed nor as reliable in their results as they are when used in the foreleg.

A surprisingly large number of horses fail to yield any clues as to the site or cause of lameness in spite of such extensive examination, which may take some time to complete and involve considerable expense, leaving the bewildered owner no further forward. In these cases a prolonged period of rest sometimes allows the horse to return to complete soundness.

7 Lower Limb Lameness, Conditions and Treatment

Hoof Wall Abnormalities

It is necessary for the hoof of the horse to be trimmed regularly to prevent excessive growth. Insufficient dressing of the hoof allows 'winging' of the hoof quarters. Once the hoof wall becomes too long leverage is increased around the margins. Portions then break off at the margin, particularly if the ground is dry and the hoof brittle. As the wall is lifted away from the sole the gap that is produced at the white line allows infection to spread inside the wall. The cracked edges allow infections to become established, resulting in pain and lameness.

Cracks may extend from the broken margin up the hoof towards the coronary band. The uninfected crack *per se* will not cause lameness unless the underlying sensory laminae are involved or unless the coronary band is reached. In these cases work may produce bleeding with or without pus formation. Cracks are generally separated into toe cracks, quarter cracks or heel cracks depending on their location in the hoof wall, but are generalised as sand or grass cracks. Occasionally, following injury to the coronary band, the crack starts at the coronet and extends down towards the ground surface. The thinner the hoof wall the greater the likelihood that cracks will develop and spread as weight is applied to the foot.

Treatment is directed towards improving the structure of the hoof wall and minimising the movement between the two edges of the crack. The structure of the hoof can be improved and the thickness and hardness increased by supplementing the diet with biotin for a period of approximately three months, with a further three months at a reduced level if required. The movement between the margins of the crack is reduced by a variety of means. If the hoof wall is lowered at the bearing surface on each side of the crack, pressure is reduced at this point. Furthermore, a bar shoe with quarter clips will prevent expansion of the hoof when weight is applied to the foot. A rasp or hot iron is commonly used to create a horizontal groove across the top of the crack to prevent it from extending further up the hoof. Although it is widely used the technique is frequently unsuccessful unless the crack is very superficial. A horse shoe nail placed horizontally across the crack and bent forward at the shank can help to stabilise the crack in less serious cases.

To achieve a lasting result the crack must be completely cleaned of any infection. Where the crack is extensive, anaesthesia of the foot using a nerve block or even general anaesthesia should precede treatment. The crack is stripped out using a small sharp hoof knife or motorised burr, without involving the sensitive

Fig 59   Cracks in the hoof wall are often multiple and may not
arise from the ground surface.

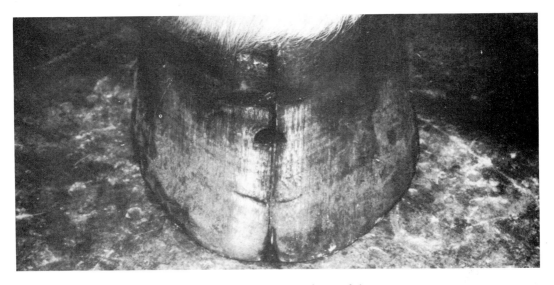

Fig 60   A hot iron placed horizontally over the top of a crack is
unlikely to prevent the crack from spreading.

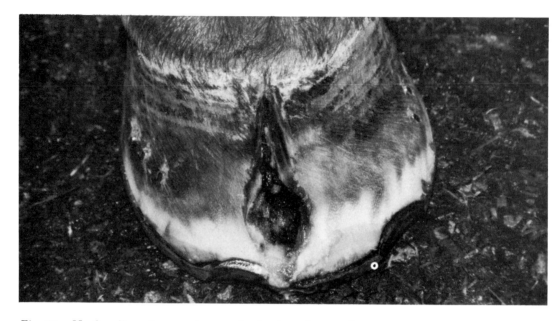

Fig 61   Hoof wall cracks must be completely cleaned out and immobilised.

laminae. The edges are then fixed together. Traditionally this has been done by lacing them using surgical wire placed through holes drilled in the hoof wall on each side of the crack. Even braided surgical wire does, however, have a tendency to cut through the hoof wall and pull out. Probably more satisfactory is the use of a strong metal plate screwed on to the surface of the hoof wall. In either case the crack can be filled with epoxy resin glue to further restrict movement between the edges. As the crack grows out the epoxy resin is rasped away from the ground surface. By providing a smooth outer surface to the hoof wall further damage or re-infection is prevented. Resin or filler can similarly be used to smooth the broken edges of the hoof where the feet are brittle, thus preventing sharp edges from catching and being torn away, or infection from becoming established in the broken cracks. Care must be taken to ensure that

no pocket of infection exists before the resin is applied, or an abscess will develop under the resin.

A fibreglass patch can be applied to the outside of the cleaned crack and held in place using short screws until the glass fibre has been allowed to harden completely. The screws are then removed and the patch rasped smooth. Where the crack involves the coronary band, stabilisation must be achieved. Once again it is vital to ensure that the area is already free of infection.

An alternative approach to treatment is to remove a wider section of hoof wall, approximately 2 cm in width, and support the sole using a heart bar shoe. This applies pressure to the frog, preventing tearing of the live laminae from the hoof wall on each side of the gap that has been created. In all cases it is necessary to ensure that the horse is protected against tetanus.

Horizontal cracks in the hoof wall

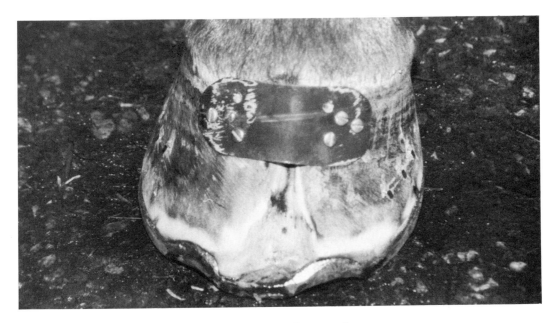

Fig 62   A metal plate can be used to immobilise the two edges of the crack.

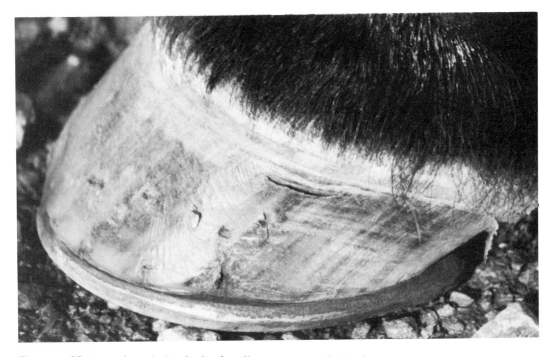

Fig 63   Horizontal cracks in the hoof wall grow out as the hoof grows.

most frequently follow injury to the coronary band or indicate the site where infection has broken out after spreading up inside the hoof wall from the solar surface. Unless extensive, they are not usually serious and grow out without problems.

It is not uncommon to find avulsion or tearing of the hoof wall at the heel. The hoof wall becomes separated from the underlying laminae just below the coronary band. Separation may be accompanied by infection and is usually the result of trauma (physical damage) although the underlying cause may be infection, a kick or prolonged foot imbalance. On occasions the condition can cause severe lameness and in these cases it

will be necessary to remove the separated portion and apply a bar shoe. An antiseptic cover should be applied until the underlying tissue has become hardened and cornified.

Following all injuries to the hoof wall in which the coronary band is involved there may be a permanent deformity in the growth of the hoof wall and corrective shoeing must be permanently applied. Where injury to the coronary band results in a lasting growth defect and abnormal horn production, an irregularity occurs in the surface of the hoof wall, extending from the coronet to the ground surface. This condition is commonly known as 'false quarter' and is a permanent feature of the hoof although

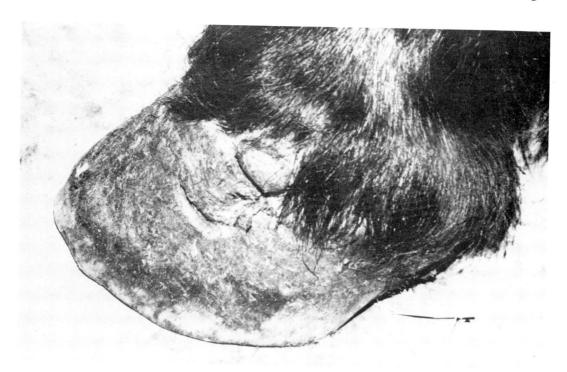

Fig 64 Damage to the coronary band leads to defects in growth of the hoof wall.

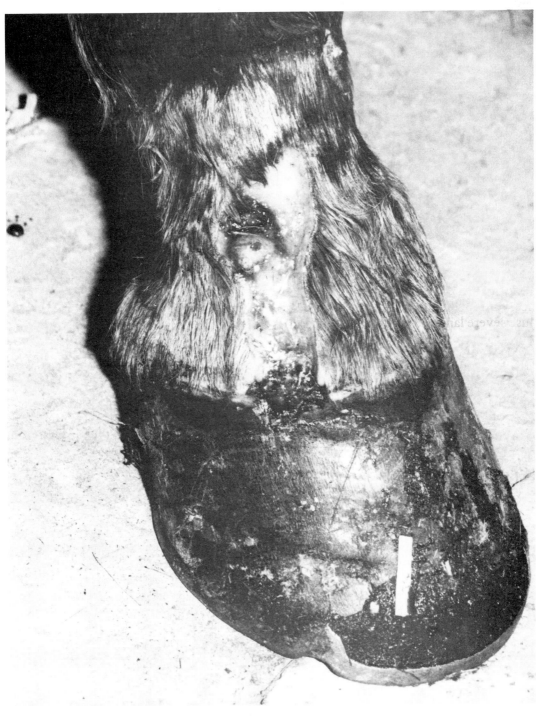

Fig 65   *If the coronary band is severely damaged, there may be
a permanent defect in horn growth.*

it does not cause lameness unless it becomes infected. The roughened surface should be smoothed with a rasp whenever the horse is shod.

Occasionally the horn of the hoof wall may proliferate as a benign tumour or keratoma on the inner aspect of the wall. It extends as a core from the ground surface up the inside of the hoof wall. The keratoma is usually found at the toe and although it can occur spontaneously, it may result from chronic irritation. Pressure on the internal structures of the foot causes progressive lameness as the tumour grows. X-radiography may demonstrate deformity of the pedal bone. The tumour will continue to grow and should be excised as quickly as possible. To do this it may be necessary to remove a section of overlying hoof wall. A shoe which provides plenty of cover, particularly at the toe, and lowering of the heels, helps to reduce pressure on the tumour. The shoe should be seated out completely at the toe to ensure that no pressure is applied to the area immediately around the keratoma.

Bruising and Infections Within the Foot

Bruising

Horses that work over rough ground are susceptible to bruising of the sole particularly when the ground is moist and the sole is soft. If the foot lands heavily on a hard, irregular surface such as a protruding stone an immediate severe lameness will occur. This may be present for only a few strides or it may be present but gradually improving over a long period of time. It might be several weeks

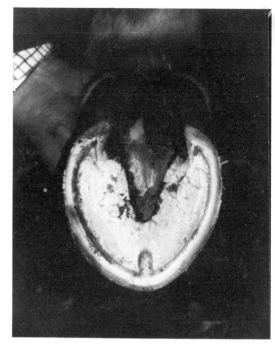

Fig 66 A keratoma is a benign tumour on the inside of the hoof wall, usually at the toe.

before a severe bruise is fully resolved. Typically, the bruised area will show as a pink mark, more easily seen in the white hoof, indicating an increased blood supply to the area with leakage of blood into the surrounding horn. Where the bruise is deep, pink discoloration may not be present on the surface for several days, although there will be a marked response to pressure applied over the bruise with hoof testers. Assuming that no infection has been introduced, the bruising will resolve spontaneously provided that the horse is kept on a smooth surface. The soles of horses that are regularly worked on rough surfaces will gradually harden and increase in resistance to bruising so that the horse will gain in confidence. The application of protective pads to the sole may prevent bruising but will also prevent the development of resistance. Thus it is preferable for the horse to travel carefully with unprotected soles across irregular surfaces.

Where bruising occurs at the toe, underneath the shoe, the horse is probably moving abnormally in bringing the toe to the ground first in an effort to protect the heel area. A thorough examination of the heels should be made to identify the underlying cause of lameness.

Corns

Sometimes bruising occurs in the angle of the foot between the hoof wall and the bar on either or both sides of the frog, although the inside is most frequently affected. Bruising at these sites is commonly called corns. Corns are much more frequently found on the forefeet particularly in the horse with flat feet. The inside heel is more usually affected since the pressure is greater here than on the outside, as the centre of gravity of the horse is midway between the legs. The common cause of corn formation is the failure of the shoes to fit the foot, a failure which generally occurs because the shoes have been left on for too long a period. The shoe is fixed to the foot at the toe so that as the foot grows the shoe is pulled forward and the heel is left unsupported. Abnormal pressure is then applied where the hoof drops over the end of the shoe. The ignorant owner attempts to leave the shoes on too long because the horse has not been in regular work and the shoe is not completely worn. This false economy results in corn formation and a lame horse. If the shoes are not excessively worn once the hoof has regrown after, say, six weeks, the shoes should be removed, the feet dressed or cut back and the shoes replaced.

The conditions that predispose to corn formation are sometimes achieved when the farrier applies a shoe that is too short or is fitted too narrow at the heels. Some farriers adopt the practice of turning both heels of the shoe towards the frog to prevent the shoe from being pulled off. As the hoof grows and the shoe is pulled forward the heel comes to lie in the angle of the bar. There is often strong pressure on the farrier by the owner to use short shoes and turn them in since it is incorrectly assumed that the horse will overreach and pull off shoes if the heels are left long. Properly safed-off shoes are unlikely to be pulled off by overreaching. When repeated over a long period this mistake results in a foot conformation which is predisposed to navicular disease.

Occasionally corns may result from the pressure of structures within the foot. The seat of corn is immediately overlain by the wing of the pedal bone. If new bone is present on the solar surface of the bone as a result of chronic concussion or chronic infection it will supply this pressure. Chronic concussion is most commonly seen in horses with a hoof/pastern axis that is broken back so that there is little space between the wings of the pedal bone and the sole, and weight on the wings is excessive. Where corns persist or recur regularly it is valuable to examine the pedal bone radiographically to ensure that early pedal ostitis is not responsible for the problem. In severe cases serum may collect under the damaged horn. Removal of the surface will relieve pressure but such surgery should not be sufficiently deep that the sensitive tissues are touched. Sometimes the corn can become infected and when this happens the infected area should be opened and drained and treated in the same manner as any other infection in the foot.

Preferably, the horse with corns should be left unshod until the lameness has ceased. Where a shoe must be fitted to the horse with a corn a shoe with a 'set' heel is not satisfactory in providing support since it does so only on the ground surface. Rather, in mild cases it is better that the shoe is lengthened to give more support, until in severe cases a full bar or egg bar shoe is indicated. Pressure on the corn can be removed by slightly lowering the surface at the seat of the corn. It is more important to ensure that in future the shoes are sufficiently long and properly fitted at the quarters.

Infections Within the Foot

Infections within the foot will take several days to reach the intensity at which they cause lameness. However, whereas the affected horse will sometimes show a lameness progressing in severity over four to five days, on other occasions the horse will deteriorate from soundness to hardly weight-bearing within a few hours. Lameness of this type can only be the result of a fractured bone or infection within the foot. If no action is taken infection will spread up the leg following the lines of least resistance around and along the lines of the tendons and ligaments. The lameness is then relieved to a degree.

Distension of the whole leg following tracking of the infection up from within the hoof must be carefully differentiated from other conditions which cause gross swelling of the leg. Mud fever occurs on the lower limb, most commonly behind the pastern, as the result of infection by the organism *Dermatophilus congolensis*, which has some characteristics of bacteria and others of fungi. These organisms attack damaged skin and cause small punctures through the full depth of the skin. Where secondary infection by bacteria occurs through these punctures the leg can rapidly become grossly swollen and intensely painful to the touch.

Fractures of the limb bones may cause a gross distension of the tissues surrounding the bones as they fill with fluid, with intense pain on manipulation of the limb. Sometimes a grating feeling (crepitus) can be appreciated as bone fragments move over each other. Unless the bones of the pastern or foot are involved, such swelling does not normally extend to the coronet and is greatest over the site of the fracture.

Severe damage to the flexor tendons or suspensory ligament behind the cannon bone will cause a similar massive swelling of the leg and can often be mistaken as the problem when infection in the foot is to blame. In this situation, however, the swelling around the pastern is minimal. A horse that is treated for damaged tendons or ligaments when the real injury is infection tracking from the foot may well find its condition seriously worsened by the incorrect treatment.

A number of abnormalities involving other systems of the body, notably heart, liver and blood vascular system may predispose to fluid accumulation under the skin in the lower limbs. When this happens the hind limbs are usually most severely involved. Furthermore the legs are not painful to the touch, there is no

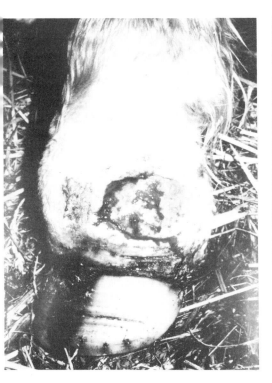

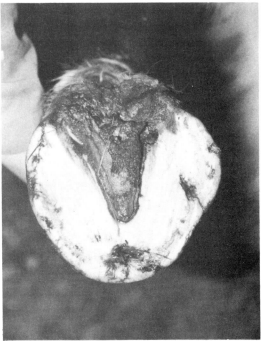

Fig 67   Incorrect treatment of soft tissue swelling of the lower limb can seriously worsen the condition.

Fig 68   Drainage of infection through a track to the sole is very beneficial in reducing infection quickly. Note the winging.

heat in the swellings and both hind legs are affected simultaneously. Perhaps of most importance is that the horse is not lame.

The horse with infection in the foot finds further relief when the infection breaks out as a discharging wound. This occurs at the first opportunity, often at the coronet immediately above the site of entry into the hoof. Some of the infected material can be removed by poulticing the wound but the effect is similar to collecting what overflows from an over-full cup. It is far more effective to empty the cup by drilling a hole in the base. Similarly, if the sole of the foot is thoroughly explored, a black track can usually be found along which the infection has entered the foot. By opening this and

creating good drainage the most rapid resolution may be achieved. Sometimes antibacterial agents may be helpful and action should always be taken to guard against tetanus.

Infections may enter the foot through a hole made in the sole by a sharp stone, piece of metal or a similar object. Sometimes a nail can be placed too near to the live laminar tissue during shoeing, a condition known as 'nail bind'. The horse will normally become lame after approximately 24 hours due to local inflammation putting pressure on the laminae. This is in distinction to pricking of the laminae when the horse will be lame immediately and blood will be seen. If the offending nail is left, infection will become established over the next four to five days before lameness becomes obvious.

When the nail is placed even further into the live tissue so that it lies inside the white line the results will be similar but much more dramatic. When the hoof/pastern axis is broken back the sensitive and non-sensitive laminae become elongated and in these cases nailing within the white line may not cause lameness.

Occasionally the horse will become lame within 24 hours of shoeing, at which time pus can be drained from the foot. In this case infection must have been brewing within the foot at the time of shoeing and the manipulation of the foot during the shoeing process has accentuated a hitherto unnoticed lameness.

Except where drainage has been achieved without removing the shoe, the horse should remain unshod until no further drainage can be achieved from the foot and the lameness has been eliminated.

Quittor   The longer that infection remains within the foot, the more extensive its effect and the more structures that are likely to become involved. When the collateral cartilages develop a chronic infection the condition is known as quittor. An alternative cause of quittor is following injury at the coronary band, most commonly through a wire injury or over-reach. Usually the cartilage on only one side of the foot is affected, causing a localised, hot, painful swelling. A discharging sinus may develop, breaking out periodically. Ultimately the area will become permanently swollen and the cartilage bony, causing lameness. Multiple sinus tracts are usually present at the coronet. The condition is most effectively resolved by surgically removing the affected cartilage.

Seedy toe   The tracking of dirt and grit under the hoof wall is a common sequel to laminitis, since destruction of the laminae in this condition results in separation of the hoof wall from the sole leaving a potential cavity. A shoe that is seated out at the toe helps to relieve pressure on the laminae. (Seedy toe will be discussed in more detail in the section on 'laminitis').

Thrush   Infection of the frog leads to a condition characterised by a black discharge of decaying material with a very unpleasant odour, usually in the hind feet. The normal consistency of the frog is rubbery, so that it is more moist than the remainder of the hoof, and bacteria are better predisposed to proliferate in airless cracks and clefts. These bacteria *Fusiformis* or *Spherophorus necrophorus* become best established in an environment devoid of oxygen but which is warm and wet. This situation is most commonly brought about by standing on dirty bedding for prolonged periods, although the presence of pads on the feet may allow accumulation of dirt beneath them and adjacent to the frog where it cannot easily be removed. The horse with thrush is not normally lame unless the infection is sufficiently severe that it affects the sensitive frog. The rubbery nature of the frog renders the area difficult to drain in the manner used for the rest of the hoof. Where the frog is contracted, as it often is in cases of thrush, the condition is more difficult still to resolve.

Once the environmental conditions are altered and a clean dry bed is provided, thrush will resolve spontaneously, but the use of astringents to dry the carefully cleaned fissures will speed recovery. Any dead frog material should first be removed.

Corrective shoeing is directed towards increasing frog pressure and increasing the size of the frog.

Sheared Heels

One condition causing lameness in the horse that can usually be attributed to poor farriery in one form or another is that of sheared heels. The term refers to the separation of the two heels which is caused when different pressures are exerted on each heel as weight is applied to the leg. Excessive use of one heel always results from chronic imbalance of the foot and leads to a variable degree of lameness. Lameness occurs when shearing is sufficiently severe that it affects the digital cushion deep to the heels so that pressure is, in turn, increased on the related, more sensitive structures. As pressure is applied to the normally balanced heel, both bulbs will become equally compressed. On the unbalanced foot, however, one heel is compressed more than the other, tearing them apart. Occasionally a deep crack forms at the central sulcus of the frog. Subsequent infection may actually result in secondary thrush being present.

Lameness is increased when the affected horse is on a hard surface. Close observation of the footfall is an accurate aid to the diagnosis of sheared heels, since one heel is more compressed than the other. A careful examination of the foot shows the over-used heel to be shorter than the normal heel on the ground surface (*see* Fig 69). The hoof with a long toe and low weak heels is particularly susceptible to this condition. The wall of

the hoof is more upright on the affected side and may even be curved underneath the foot, while that on the normal side is flared. If the heels are manipulated they are found to move separately in a vertical, rotationary plane. Such manipulation produces evidence of pain.

Shearing of the heels arises from imbalance of the foot, but imbalance can be caused by a number of factors:

1. The most common cause is the use of large studs in one heel of the shoe, usually the outer heel. This throws the weight on to the opposite heel and in the long term can lead to shearing. Although some form of anti-slip device is often needed, one with a low profile, such as a stud nail will be equally effective and much less harmful. If stud nails are placed in both heels, the weight distribution will be even and the forces equally distributed.
2. When more hoof is rasped off one heel than the other when the hoof is dressed, shearing may result. The right-handed farrier is inclined to rasp more off the outer heel of the left foot and the inner heel of the right foot. This is easily done and leaves one side of the foot lower than the other.
3. In the normal horse the branches of the shoe must come into contact with the ground together. In the majority of cases when a shoe is fitted in which the branches are of different lengths, the heel will drop on the side with the short branch and the forces are again unevenly distributed. Occasionally it is necessary to fit heels of unequal length in order that they do meet the ground together.
4. Any attempt to correct a longstanding conformational defect of a limb will, inevitably, throw the balanced foot out of balance in the early stages. Consequently

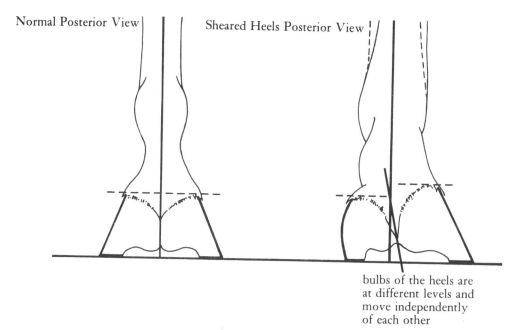

Fig 69   Sheared heels.

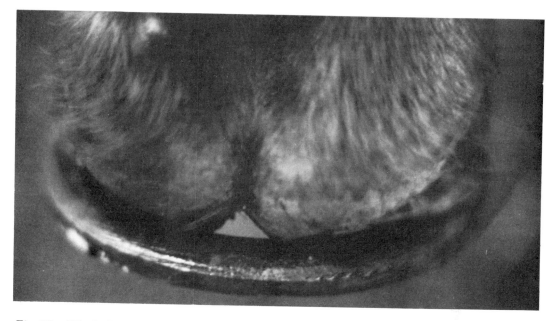

Fig 70   The bulbs of the heel can be supported using the egg bar shoe.

there is a risk that sheared heels will occur as a side-effect.

Unfortunately, since the condition is the product of poor farriery, it is likely that the same farrier will not be too conscientious about correcting the problem. If correction is carried out carefully there is a very good chance of complete and rapid recovery. In mild cases it is necessary only to level and balance the foot, but in more severe cases a full bar or egg bar shoe will serve to fix the bulbs of the heel together.

Fractures of the Lower Limb

Fractures of the bones of the limb below the fetlock are relatively rare. Such fractures are by no means irreparable although the prospect of the horse returning to full working soundness depends on the site of the fracture, the manner in which it is repaired and the type of work to which the horse may be returned. A horse that is sound enough to hunt, for example, may show sufficient shortening of its stride to render it unsuitable for use as a dressage horse.

In general, fractures involving the bones of the hind limbs are more successfully repaired than those of the forelimbs. This is because the hind limbs carry less weight than the forelimbs, a feature which is exaggerated when the horse is landing after jumping.

Fractures that do not involve a joint surface or do not show displacement of the broken fragments are much more likely to heal successfully.

Third Phalanx (Pedal Bone)

Surprisingly, probably the most common bone to be fractured is the third (distal) phalanx or pedal bone. This is unexpected because the bone is enclosed by the strongly protective covering of the hoof. Nevertheless, as the foot lands on a protruding stone during galloping, or after similar trauma, there may be sufficient distortion of the sole to cause the underlying bone to fracture. Similarly, a violent kick against a solid and sharp object may cause the hind pedal bone to fracture. Where horses are galloped on hard surfaces in a circle, fractures may occur on the inside of the pedal bone of the inside leg. A twisting action as the foot hits the ground may result in a fracture of the pedal bone. Occasionally the tip of the pedal bone may fracture after chronic infection around the bone has caused infection within the bone (osteomyelitis). This sometimes occurs as a sequel to toxic laminitis.

Where the fracture extends to the coffin joint it must be surgically immobilised using screws across the fracture. No movement is admissible and alignment must be perfect to prevent permanent arthritis from ensuing.

More frequently, one wing of the bone may become fractured. Clearly, displacement can only be slight and often treatment is to immobilise the bone from the outside, using the hoof as a splint. Normally the hoof wall expands as weight is applied to the foot. Following such a fracture, expansion is prevented by application of a bar shoe and quarter clips around the wall so that the whole structure remains rigid. A full sole plate provides further rigidity. The clips should extend well up the wall of the hoof.

Expansion of the foot at the heels can be further reduced by supplying a sling support under the fetlock to retard its descent.

Occasionally the extensor process is fractured and an enlargement can be detected which is painful on manipulation at the coronary band at the front of the hoof. It is best that the chip of bone is surgically removed. Sometimes such fractures can occur in both forefeet simultaneously, usually as the result of excessive tension on the extensor tendon which attaches to the process and pulls the process off. Conservative treatment is prolonged and has limited success.

Second Phalanx

Fractures of the second (middle) phalanx or short pastern bone are rare in the United Kingdom but relatively common in the United States. The bone is short and squat and able to withstand enormous compressive forces that may be applied to it. Fractures are largely confined to the hind limbs of middle-aged horses that are required to make sudden turns on their hind quarters so that there are tremendous rotational forces on the bone. Consequently, horses that are involved in cutting, barrel racing and, to a lesser extent, show jumping are the most susceptible. The presence of large studs or calkins increases the risk of such a fracture occurring. Frequently the bone splits into several pieces.

Unlike fractures of the pedal bone, fractures of the middle phalanx render the horse unable to bear weight unless only a small chip has fractured from the bone. Manipulation of the foot will usually cause obvious pain and grating (crepitation) at the site of the fracture.

The approach to treatment and likelihood of full recovery depends, again, on whether joints are involved and the complexity of the fracture. External fixation by casting can be successful in a few cases but most require surgical screwing of the bone fragments. Where many bone fragments are present casting is the most successful form of treatment but where the coffin (distal interphalangeal) joint is involved chances of return to full work are very poor.

First Phalanx

The first (proximal) phalanx is more commonly fractured than the second phalanx due to the waisted shape of the bone. Fractures tend to run longitudinally down the bone and to involve joint surfaces or adopt an oblique course across one corner. Racing thoroughbreds frequently sustain simple longitudinal fractures, producing the 'split pastern', in which lameness can be surprisingly mild. After a short period of rest the affected horse may become sound, only to revert to lameness on return to work. Where the fracture is multiple and complex it usually follows sudden turning on the leg and leaves the impression on manipulation that you are handling a bag of marbles. In this situation the horse is unable to bear weight on the foot.

Fractures of the first phalanx may be treated by casting but if return to full work is expected, surgical internal fixation is far more likely to produce satisfactory healing.

Navicular Bone

Fractures of the distal sesamoid or navicular bone are rare. Although fractures may occur as a sequel to severe navicular disease they are more likely to follow trauma to the foot as, for example, when a solid object has been kicked. Displacement of the bone fragments is slight due to the protected position of the bone, but immobilisation is difficult for the same reason. Multiple fractures are even less common.

The clinical signs produced by such fractures closely resemble the more acute cases of navicular disease and great care is needed to differentiate the two conditions.

Although fixation of the foot with a bar shoe and quarter clips in the manner described for fracture of the pedal bone may be beneficial, surgical repair of the fracture by screwing provides a considerably more stable fracture site.

Splints

Bony enlargements are not uncommon on the sides and behind the cannon bones of the fore or hind limb. These enlargements are usually all termed 'splints' although many are not. Any direct blow to the cannon bone will cause bleeding under the skin-like periosteum that covers the bone. The enlargement that results rapidly becomes hard and bony, taking months to reduce in size and fine down. Provided that the enlargement does not cause tension on any overlying tendon or ligament, and does not directly affect the carpal or knee joint the horse will not be lame. The same applies to the splint, although in some horses lameness may result during the time at which the splint is forming.

A splint is a bony outgrowth between the cannon bone and one or other of the splint bones (the second or fourth metacarpal or metatarsal bones) of the fore or hind leg. The two adjacent bones are joined by the interosseous ligament, and if this is torn, a splint forms. The interosseous ligament has become ossified by about five years of age, taking on the properties of bone, so that after this time tearing cannot occur. Consequently splints do not normally occur once the change has taken place, but identical clinical signs can be seen when the splint bone is fractured. There is some evidence to support the contention that a relative calcium deficiency or phosphorus excess in the diet, as is produced by high levels of bran or cereals, prevents complete ossification of the ligament and renders tearing more likely during work.

A splint normally occurs as a single swelling or a line of swellings approximately 7 – 8cm below the knee, although swellings may sometimes be present immediately below the joint. It should be remembered that the splint bone usually has a 'button' on the lower tip which may be confused as a bony enlargement due to a splint. In the forelimb splints are more common on the inside (medial) splint bone due to the anatomical relationship with the knee. The second carpal bone sits above the head of the medial splint bone, whereas the lateral splint bone on the outside is covered by the fourth carpal bone which also extends over the cannon bone, thereby providing greater stability. During fast work on hard surfaces abnormal weight distribution on to the knee joint pushes the second carpal bone downwards, tearing it from the cannon. The effect is exacerbated by the greater force being passed down the inside of the joint since the centre of gravity of the horse lies inside (medial to) the entire leg.

97

Splints are more common on the outside of the hind leg as a result of increased pressure placed on the outside of the joint by the horse that screws the hind foot as it hits the ground. The use of a large calkin or stud on the outside of the shoe accentuates the screwing action. The chances of traumatic injury to the splint bone are increased in the horse that stands with the toe out and consequently moves close, and where incorrect shoeing or trimming alters the flight pattern of the foot.

Initially there is localised pain and swelling during splint formation and lameness may be present. Once the inflammation subsides, lameness remains only when the swelling interferes with the action of the knee, flexor tendons or the suspensory ligaments. Usually the splint remains only as a blemish, fining down over about nine months from a discrete enlargement to become elongated, tapering at the ends.

It is customary to rest a horse during the period until the primary inflammation has subsided after several weeks. If it is necessary to continue to work the horse further, concussion must be minimised by applying a pad between the shoe and the foot. The period that the foot is on the ground is minimised by rolling the toe and raising the heel. Usually, though, it is unnecessary to take any action as the swelling has no functional significance.

Sidebone

The importance of sidebone as a cause of lameness in the horse has been traditionally exaggerated. It is a perfectly normal phenomenon that as a horse ages the cartilages that extend upwards from the wings of the pedal bone should become ossified or bony. The condition of sidebone is progressive until the point at which the whole cartilage has become ossified. Consequently the natural flexibility of the cartilages is progressively lost and they become hard and firm. The change can be appreciated by pressing the foot above the coronary band above the bulbs of the heels. The normal springy feel is replaced by a firm bony feeling. Such a change may occur quite early in life, particularly in the heavier breeds of horse. The formation of sidebones follows concussion of the quarters of the feet which is greater in the forefeet, to which sidebone is usually confined. The use of large studs in the shoe over a prolonged period may exacerbate the process. Alternatively, where the foot is not dressed level the weight may be thrown on to one side of the foot. There is little evidence to support the belief that the condition is inherited although the poor conformation that pushes the weight on to either the outside or the inside of the foot may be hereditary.

Occasionally the cartilage is damaged by direct trauma such as that which occurs when wire wounds cause injury to the area.

On the rare occasions in which lameness results from the formation of sidebones, pain is produced by the pressure of the firm structures on the overlying sensitive coronary band and compression of the sensitive internal structures of the hoof wall. Sometimes the ossification occurs on only one side of the foot. When lameness does result from sidebone formation it is nearly always associated with rapid ossification of the cartilage and is mild, showing only on the turn. The horse will flinch to pressure on the area.

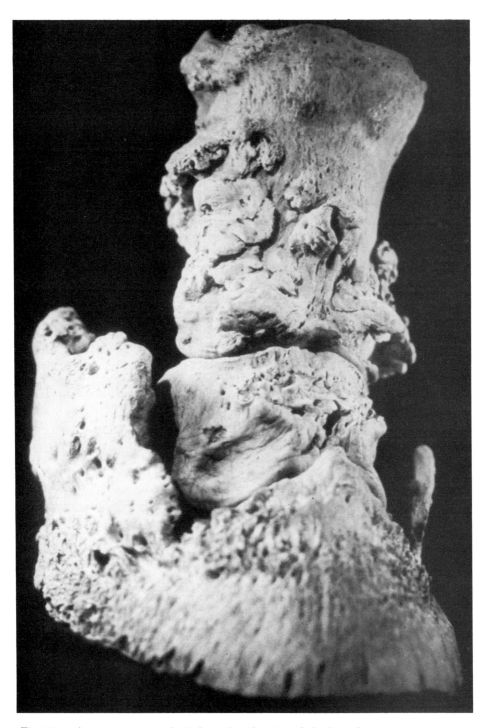

Fig 71 An extreme case of sidebone (ossification of the lateral cartilages).

Ossification does not continue from the margin of the cartilage that is attached to the pedal bone and spread in a wave form up the cartilage, but begins from a separate centre near the top (proximal) margin of the cartilage and extends in a radiating fashion until it reaches the pedal bone. If X-radiographs are taken of the area before the process is complete, the new bone will be visible but a line of cartilage between the ossified cartilage and the pedal bone will not. The apparent separation may easily lead to the mistaken assumption that the sidebone has been fractured from the pedal bone. On rare occasions the sidebone does fracture causing a more severe lameness. In these cases the fractured portion should be surgically removed.

When sidebone does cause lameness, treatment is directed towards allowing the hoof wall to expand over the ossified area. This is done by making vertical grooves in the hoof wall to permit the foot to expand. Alternatively flexibility of the hoof wall can be increased by rasping the outer surface of the hoof wall to produce thinning although this may help the hoof wall to become distorted in the long term. By applying a shoe with a rolled toe minimal movement in the coffin joint is achieved. Normally, where sidebone is present, the outer edge of the shoe on the affected side becomes excessively worn. The therapeutic shoe to be applied should have a long heel to spread the load over the maximum area. The web of the shoe is also widened.

Joint Diseases

Ringbone

Heavier horses, especially those that have an upright conformation, are very susceptible to concussion through the lower joints of the forelimb. Tearing of the ligaments surrounding the pastern and coffin (proximal and distal interphalangeal) joints at their points of attachment to the bones results in a local reaction at these points and the formation of new bone. A similar effect can result from the tearing of attachments to the extensor tendons, or from trauma to the area such as from blows or wire cuts. Where the formation of new bone extends across the joints, movement is restricted and painful. This condition is recognised as true ringbone in contradistinction to the formation of new bone on the long or short pastern bones (proximal or middle phalanges) which does not involve the joints and which is known as false ringbone.

True ringbone is further classified into high and low ringbone depending on whether the pastern or coffin joint space is affected. Normally the surface on the inside of the joint is affected in ringbone and in those cases where the inside is not involved the term *periarticular ringbone* is used.

Whereas heavier horses are more susceptible to false and periarticular ringbone, true ringbone is more common in horses that turn quickly during their work, thereby increasing the shearing forces on the joints. Degenerative joint disease, in which the major pathological processes take place within the joint, sometimes occurs in the young horse before it begins work, most frequently in the pastern joint of one or both hind

100

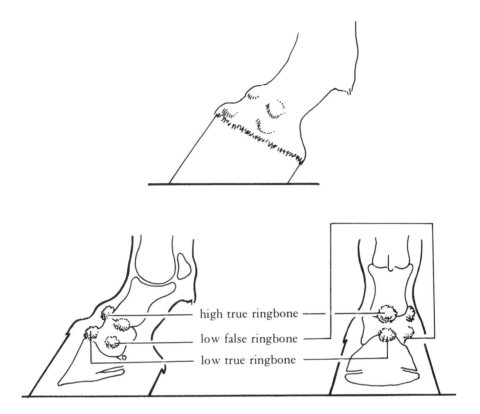

high true ringbone

low false ringbone

low true ringbone

Fig 72   Sites of ringbone formation.

limbs. The condition is probably inherited only by virtue of the fact that the poor conformation that produces the abnormal stresses that lead to such degenerative changes is inheritable.

Lameness caused by ringbone is marked and usually progressive. It is characterised by a gait in which the foot is placed heel first on the ground. In severe cases bony swellings may be felt in the pastern region. They must, however, be differentiated radiographically from false ringbones which may not cause lameness. Where false ringbone does cause lameness it is through interference with the overlying soft tissue structures such as the extensor tendon on the anterior surface of the pastern.

If new bone forms following tearing of the attachment of the extensor tendon from the pedal bone (third phalanx) a marked enlargement may be present at the front of the coronary band, producing a buttress foot. Heat, swelling and pain may be present at the site of new bone formation.

The treatment of ringbone is aimed at minimising movement of the affected joint as much as possible. In the early stages this can be done by prolonged periods of rest, and the horse may even benefit from having the foot placed in a cast. Once the affected joint has become fused the horse will cease to be lame although its action may be restricted. Often, however, such fusion does not

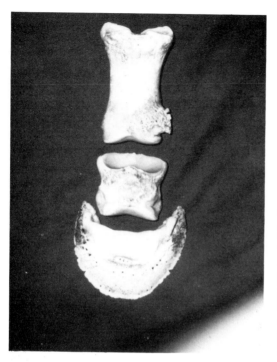

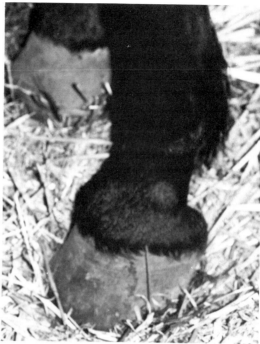

Fig 73 *Periarticular new bone (false ringbone) is common in heavier horses following traumatic injury to the pastern.*

Fig 74 *Ringbone and false ringbone may be visible as a bony swelling, or may require radiography for identification.*

occur and massive new bone formation occurs around the joint. Surgical fusion of such joints is necessary. This form of treatment is not satisfactory where the coffin (distal interphalangeal) joint is involved.

As with other forms of treatment, the purpose of shoeing is to help the horse to progress with minimal movement of the joints of the lower limb. In very mild cases the shoe is lowered at the heels to correspond to the wear that is found on normal shoes on the affected horse. In more severe cases a rolled toe or even a full roller action shoe is used to maximise the ease with which breakover can occur.

Bone Spavin

The hock joint (tarsus) is extremely complex, involving ten bones. Most of these occur in two rows immediately above (proximal to) the cannon bone. There is little movement between these bones when the hock joint is moved but the individual joints are very susceptible to abnormal stresses, and degenerative joint disease and osteoarthritis may ensue. Such a condition is commonly called bone spavin. Bone spavin most frequently affects the bottom two joints of the hock (the distal intertarsal and tarsometatarsal joints). When the next joint up the leg (the proximal intertarsal joint) is affected the chance of complete recovery is reduced due to the greater

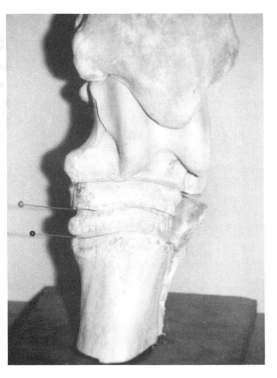

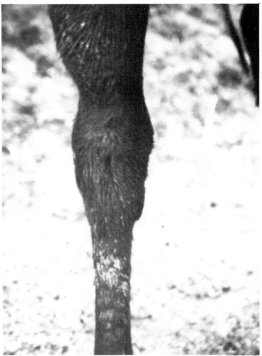

Fig 75   The most common sites of bone spavin formation in the hock joint.

Fig 76   Severe bone spavin is visible as a bony swelling on the inside of the hock.

movement within the joint. In more advanced stages the condition is characterised by increased formation of new bone, particularly on the front and inside aspects of the joint, until finally all movement of the joint is stopped as the new bone forms a bridge and prevents any movement. If this is done without too much new bone forming on the outside the horse will no longer feel pain on flexion of the joint, although movement may be mechanically reduced.

Insidious in onset, the condition may result in severe lameness and a large bony swelling which is known as a jack spavin, visible on the inside of the hock. It is most commonly found in mature horses that are used for jumping and turning suddenly. The horse with cow hocks is more susceptible to the condition since

further strains are applied to the abnormal joint during activity. Sickle hocks or straight hocks are also frequently affected by bone spavin. In some young horses spavin may be a sequel to dietary deficiency, imbalance of calcium, phosphorus, or vitamins A or D, or excessive protein intake.

Initially, lameness may be intermittent and disappear with rest or it may even be absent, the only sign being poor jumping performance for no apparent reason. In the early stages, any lameness may disappear once the horse has warmed into its work. Usually bone spavin affects both hocks although not necessarily to the same degree.

Forced flexion of the hock joint causes increased severity of the lameness, although other conditions of the hock and stifle joints may produce a similar or even more severe response. X-radiographic examination may show formation of new bone on the anterior and medial (inner) aspects of the appropriate joints, but this is not always the case. Where changes are confined to within the joint, damage to the cartilaginous surfaces will allow the joint to become widened with irregular edges, before becoming narrowed and finally obliterated. Such subtle changes will not be appreciated unless the radiographs are of the highest quality and the X-ray beam is centred on the joint in question and directed in exactly the same plane as the joint. Where the diagnosis is still in doubt, infiltration of the joints with local anaesthetic will lead the examiner to a definite conclusion.

Bone spavin is a progressive condition so the prospect of complete resolution and elimination of pain is guarded and depends on halting the process in the very early stages of the disease or fusion of the affected joint without an excess of new bone forming on the outside of the joint. The process can be accelerated in mild cases by working the horse while giving prolonged treatment with pain-reducing drugs if required. In severe cases surgical destruction of the joint surfaces using an orthopaedic drill will hasten fusion. Excessive new bone on the outside of the joint may interfere with the cunean tendon which crosses the area obliquely, causing pain. Surgical removal of a piece of the tendon may help to reduce this pain.

The horse that has a bone spavin, even after complete fusion of the affected joint or joints, fails to flex the hock properly during movement so that the toe is dragged and touches down first as the foot hits the ground. Consequently, to reduce the wear as much as possible a shoe is fitted in which the toe is shortened and rolled to help breakover. The heels are raised by using sloping wedge shaped heels. This effect cannot be more simply produced by using a squared calkin since this would increase the drag on the heel, a feature that is highly undesirable.

Pedal Ostitis

There is a certain amount of debate regarding whether pedal ostitis (pedal osteitis) even exists as a clinical entity. The characteristic features of the condition are a thinning of the pedal bone (distal phalanx) around the margin at the toe, causing an irregularity in outline, together with an increase of bone on the solar surface at the wings of the pedal bone. When the pedal bone is viewed radiographically from the side in profile, an irregular projection of bone can be seen to extend downwards towards the ground surface in the region of the heels. The blood vascular supply to the pedal bone can, however, leave the toe of the bone with a slightly irregular appearance in normal horses and it is difficult to decide whether the irregularity that is visible is abnormal.

The pathological changes described result from chronic inflammation within the foot. The angle of the foot between the bar and the hoof wall lies immediately over the wing of the pedal bone. Consequently a chronic inflammation in this area, as is seen with persistent corns, will cause local inflammation in the adjacent bone and rough new bone is formed. The process occurs more quickly if infection results in local abscessation.

Once new bone has been formed at the heels, the process is reversed and the rough surface irritates the seat of corn. Local bruising results in persistent corn formation. The possibility of the presence of pedal ostitis should therefore be considered in horses where there is persistent recurrence of corns in spite of correct and regular shoeing. Damage at the toe may result from concussion and bruising in cases in which the horse places its toe on the ground first, either to protect the heel area when pain is present in this area (as is the case in horses with navicular disease or thrush), or where the pedal bone points downward at the tip at too sharp an angle. This is often the case in chronic laminitis or in horses with 'contracted tendons' involving the deep flexor tendon. Pedal ostitis may simply follow any of the conditions mentioned. The affected horse will show pain when pressure is applied over the pedal bone. Radiographs are necessary to substantiate a diagnosis of this condition.

Pedal ostitis is not satisfactorily treated either medically or surgically so that, particularly where signs have been present for some time, the chance of reversing the process is small. Treatment is therefore aimed at reducing the pressure on the sole as much as possible. A pad of leather or neolite under the shoe will help to absorb concussion. Rest or working on a soft surface will also help the inflammation to subside. Wide-webbed shoes will normally be fitted and seated out to reduce any pressure on the sole of the foot.

Laminitis

During the last few years laminitis has probably been the most widely researched abnormality involving the horse's foot. In consequence, radical developments have occurred in our understanding of the disease processes and in our approach to their treatment. The concept of the fat pony on lush spring grass who develops 'fever in the feet' due to a massive inflammation or increase in blood-supply in the laminae is now recognised to be in part a gross oversimplification of the facts and in certain aspects to be completely incorrect.

Laminitis is a multifactorial condition which has a variety of causes and a spectrum of clinical manifestations. Certainly the overweight pony that is allowed to have an unrestricted supply of spring grass will develop laminitis, but the condition occurs more frequently during the autumn flush of grass growth and may occur during a wet summer when grass growth rate continues to be rapid. Moreover, ponies that suffer in this way tend to be the less severely affected animals. Far more serious is the laminitis that follows engorgement by the horse or pony of excessive quantities of concentrate feed after breaking into a supply, or the toxic laminitis that follows the retention of foetal membranes, even in very small quantities, after foaling.

To discover why such problems are reflected in an abnormality in the feet we must consider the processes which lead to laminitis. Sudden dietary increase in carbohydrate intake usually in the form of grain (wheat, barley or maize) results in a change in the degree of acidity in the horse's gut and a change in the type of bacteria that develop in such an environment. The sudden increase in carbohydrate intake may be deliberate, following sudden access to lush grass or increased feeding of concentrate in a horse being prepared for showing, or accidental following breaking into a feed supply. Under such conditions these bacteria release poisonous substances (toxins) which are absorbed into the bloodstream of the horse. The reaction that they produce here damages the walls of the blood-vessels. Such a reaction causes the horse's blood-pressure to rise by causing the smaller blood-vessels (the capillaries) to contract, a phenomenon known as 'toxic shock'. Consequently, although more blood is passed to the foot, it by-passes the laminae, whose blood-supply is actually reduced. This phenomenon has been demonstrated by angiographic studies in which a radio-opaque dye has been injected into the arterial system and X-radiographs used to demonstrate the distribution of the marker and hence the blood.

Such toxin will produce the same response, regardless of the source, so that toxins produced in rotting retained foetal membranes after foaling may cause laminitis. Such toxins in small quantities are normally removed by the liver but in the fat pony much of the liver tissue may be occupied by fat deposits so that the efficiency of the liver is grossly reduced and the effect of the toxins is more prolonged.

Increase in blood-pressure may also occur following imbalance in levels of certain minerals in the horse, notably of calcium and phosphorus, sodium and potassium. These minerals are responsible for the actions of the muscles in the walls of the blood-vessels. These muscles control blood flow by altering their dia-

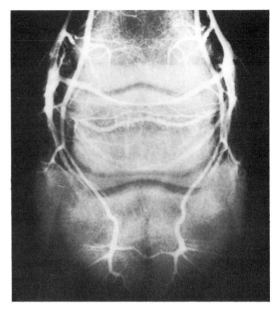

Fig 77   *The blood-supply to the foot is severely reduced during laminitis.*

meter. Relative deficiencies of these minerals can result in paralysis of the muscles.

A variety of hormones also affect blood-pressure so that a change in certain hormones will trigger laminitis. These hormonal changes most notably follow stressful situations or shock. One situation in which the hormone levels are thus abnormal is following abdominal surgery.

The reduction in blood-supply to the laminae results in reduced supply of oxygen and nutrients which are essential for the rapid growth of these tissues. Inevitably, death of the laminae, swelling, bleeding and gas formation occur under the hoof wall. This tissue destruction is acutely painful and is analogous to that experienced in the fingers during frost-bite. Pain triggers the release of

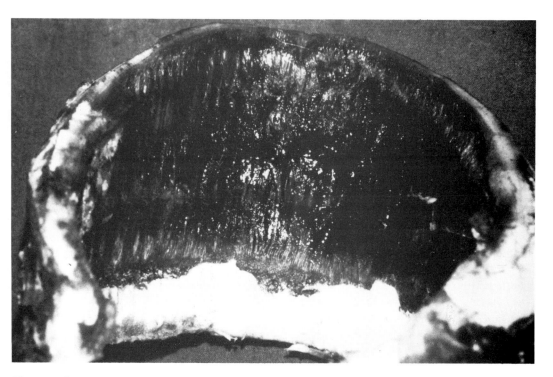

Fig 78 Severe destruction of the horny laminae results from reduction of the blood-supply and death of the tissues.

hormones which cause constriction of blood-vessels, further reducing the supply of blood to the area. Increased coagulation of blood within the blood-vessels probably increases the problem. Increase in blood-pressure may remain for up to six months after the onset of laminitis.

One further complication may be the introduction of infection into the dead tissue, either along the laminae from the ground surface, or from the blood-supply. Such infection is particularly difficult to control since the blood-supply which helps to introduce antibiotics to the area and to remove dead tissue is reduced.

The pedal bone (distal phalanx) is normally slung from the overlying wall of the hoof by the interdigitating sensitive and non-sensitive laminae. If these are destroyed by inadequate blood-supply the support to the pedal bone is lost and separation from the hoof wall follows. The weight of the horse on the bony column of the leg causes the pedal bone to be torn away (*see* Fig 79). Since the coffin (distal interphalangeal) joint is normally fixed, the centre of the joint acts as a fulcrum around which the free toe of the pedal bone rotates in a vertical plane so that it comes to apply pressure from above on to the sole (*see* Fig 80). Rotation is increased by accumulation of debris and gas between the hoof wall and the pedal bone, since there is no means by which it can be removed, and by tension applied to the underside (solar surface) of the pedal bone by the deep flexor tendon which attaches here.

The pressure of the tip of the pedal

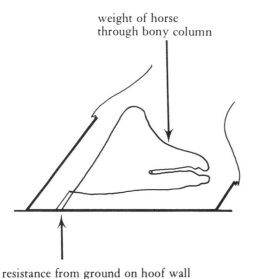

weight of horse
through bony column

resistance from ground on hoof wall
pulls hoof well away from pedal bone

*Fig 79   Normal forces applied to
the foot.*

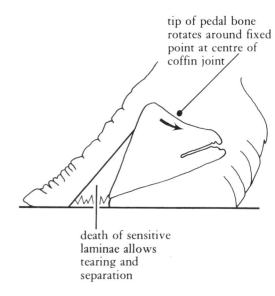

tip of pedal bone
rotates around fixed
point at centre of
coffin joint

death of sensitive
laminae allows
tearing and
separation

*Fig 80   Rotation of the pedal bone
during laminitis.*

bone on the sole can be sufficiently great that the sole is destroyed and the tip of the pedal bone penetrates it completely, in an arc in front of the point of the frog. If gas builds up between the hoof wall and the pedal bone (seroma formation), it must find an outlet. If the sole is not penetrated and no action is taken to create an outlet, the gas will escape at the point of least resistance, at the coronary band. A crack will form at the corium where the attachment of the hoof wall has died and the entire hoof may be shed, leaving the pedal bone completely exposed.

In particularly severe cases, especially in heavy horses, all the attachments between the bony column and the hoof capsule may become detached so that, instead of the pedal bone rotating, the whole column moves downwards inside the hoof capsule while maintaining a relatively straight line of bone from the pastern downwards. The whole movement can easily be overlooked even though the 'sinker' is in reality the most serious of all the eventualities.

Although laminitis is more common in ponies, it is more severe in horses. All breeds are affected but laminitis is most common in the Shetland and Welsh pony and least common in the Arab and Thoroughbred. It most commonly affects both forefeet of ponies but appears to more seriously affect the hind feet of horses. However, any combination of feet may be affected.

In the early stages, the signs of laminitis in the horse may not be at all clear. When the forefeet are the most seriously affected the animal adopts a posture in which the pressure is removed from the toes and restricted to the heels by pushing the forefeet out in front and taking the majority of weight on the hind quarters. The weight may be shifted from one hind foot to the other and back, making the horse appear to paddle. There may be abnormally frequent or prolonged periods of lying down, sweating and other evidence of pain. At this time the condition may resemble colic and, indeed, laminitis may be a sequel to colic. When made to walk or trot the horse will have a short, pottery gait but will not necessarily show overt lameness.

If we closely examine the foot, which

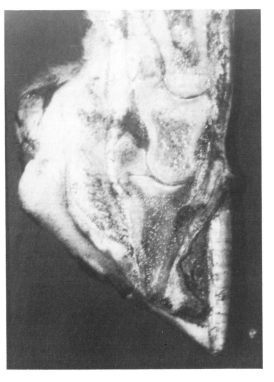

Fig 81   Rotation of the pedal bone, placing pressure on the sole. Gas and debris are present between the dorsal surface of the bone and the dorsal hoof wall.

may be very difficult in itself since persuading the animal to stand on three legs may be very awkward, we find that in the early stages heat is present within the whole hoof and coronary band area but quickly, as the laminae die, the hoof becomes cold and heat is restricted to the coronary band. In many cases the owner, and sometimes the veterinary surgeon and farrier will overlook laminitis if the feet are not hot.

After approximately 48 hours the condition moves into a more chronic phase. The laminae start to tear and the pedal bone begins to rotate. Pressure on the sole of the foot from above causes it to become flattened. Destruction of horn-forming tissue at the coronary band may, over a period of up to several weeks cause a separation of the hoof wall from the skin. Separation is accompanied by the oozing of serum and may spread from the starting point, usually above the toe, right around the coronet causing the hoof to slough from the foot. The reduction in blood-supply at the toe area of the coronary band is also responsible for the slowing of growth rate at the toe compared with that at the heel, a fact that is demonstrated by rings of hoof growth which are closer together at the toe and which diverge towards the heels. Such 'laminitic rings' should not be confused with parallel rings that occur sometimes in the normal hoof wall. The latter simply denote a change in growth rate of the entire hoof wall, as often happens when the horse is placed on a new diet. This is, of course, often precisely when laminitis occurs.

A further confusing factor is that because the horse or pony adopts a stance with the weight on the heels, the toe grows longer, albeit more slowly, before

109

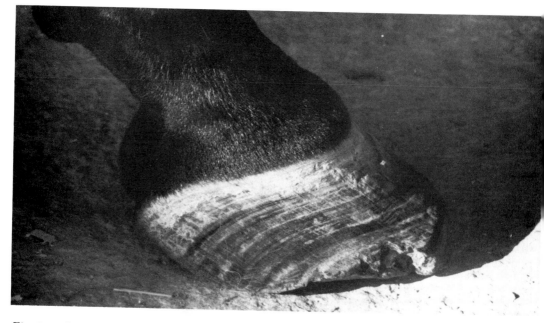

Fig 82   Growth rings on the hoof wall diverge at the heels
where growth is more rapid during laminitis.

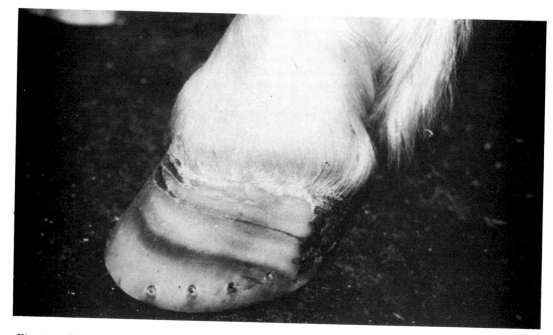

Fig 83   'Jamming' of the horn tubules at the coronet during
laminitis results in severe bruising around the hoof, which
gradually grows out.

reaching the ground, leaving the impression that it is growing more quickly at the toe. In fact, as the toe lengthens it is levered upwards during walking, which further tears the hoof wall away from the pedal bone. Also more pressure is placed on the coronary band at the toe region due to the mechanical 'jamming' effect, and this further reduces the rate of regrowth of horn. The debris that accumulates between the rotated pedal bone and the hoof wall, together with a thick layer of white scar tissue over the surface of the pedal bone, act as a wedge which keeps the hoof wall and pedal bone apart and accentuates the long toe. Such an area is visible on the ground surface as a very wide white line behind the hoof wall. The dead tissue results in the white line becoming crumbly, a condition commonly known as seedy toe. The expanse of cheesy white line is particularly susceptible to infection spreading up under the hoof wall. Over a prolonged period of time the shape of the foot completely alters so that in profile it is long at the toe and from the solar surface it appears long and narrowed.

It needs to be understood from the outset that laminitis is a potentially fatal condition and should therefore be treated as an emergency. Treatment is aimed in three directions:

1. The prevention of further damage by the removal of the cause. In animals where laminitis follows a single large intake of highly concentrated feed, a large quantity of laxative will help to remove the offending material as quickly as possible. Where laminitis results from retention of the placenta after foaling, manual removal of any remaining portions will be helpful.

Affected animals should be housed and maintained on a diet of hay and water. Complete starvation will result in the rapid breakdown of large quantities of body fat which, by overloading the liver, will create more serious problems.

2. The re-establishment of the blood-supply to the laminae. In the early stages of the condition blood circulation in the feet may be improved by forcing the animal to walk. This needs to be done frequently for short periods of five to ten minutes, not continuously for prolonged periods. Once the pedal bone has started to rotate, exercise will hasten the damage and walking should be discontinued. Walking is best done on a smooth soft surface. The horse should be bedded on a soft surface that will provide support for the whole sole area. Peat is ideal but sawdust, shredded paper or sand are quite suitable. In the past it has been the custom to stand the laminitic pony in cold water to reduce the heat in the feet. The effect of this is to reduce the blood supply to the area and the practice should be avoided.

Various medical treatments are available for use in combination with altered management to control the toxic effect, reduce the pain that the animal experiences and increase the blood flow to the feet. Where laminitis results from a septicaemic cause it is often wise also to give antibiotic treatment. If infection should spread to the bone (osteomyelitis) control is much more difficult. When lameness is severe, the use of local anaesthetics to block the nerve supply to the feet can be beneficial on humanitarian grounds. It is important to remember that once the pain is relieved by such perineural analgesia the horse will be able to walk freely and in cases where the pedal bone has started to rotate further damage may

111

result from tearing of the laminae due to movement.

3. Prevention of the long term sequelae. The most important long term result of laminitis is the rotation of the pedal bone(s). Rotation starts within hours of onset of lameness and steps can be taken to minimise it. It is important to monitor changes using X-radiography although rotation can be roughly gauged from the degree of depression that can be felt at the front of the corium. Support of the sole using a deep soft bed will help to give strength to the underlying bone. The sole should not be covered, however, unless the state of the foot is so severe that a full sole plate is necessary, since it is vital to become aware as soon as the sole has been penetrated by the rotating pedal bone. Such an important event is frequently followed by infection around the exposed tip of the pedal bone and may result in the formation of new bone at the tip, greatly reducing the chance of full return to normal work.

The most important aspect of treatment of the chronic laminitic horse or pony is in the management of the feet. To ensure full recovery, such care is critical and

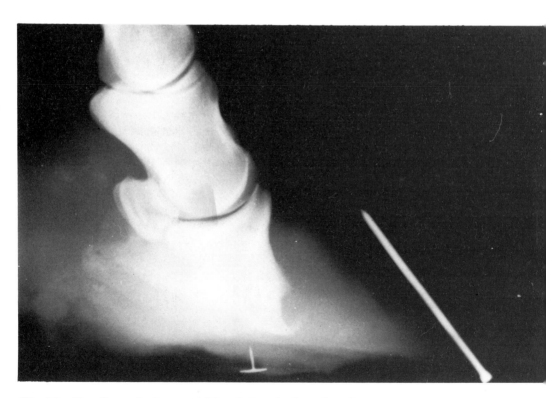

Fig 84 X-radiography is essential in placing the heart bar shoe in the correct position. Markers define the dorsal hoof wall and the point of the frog. Note the bone spicules on the tip of the pedal bone.

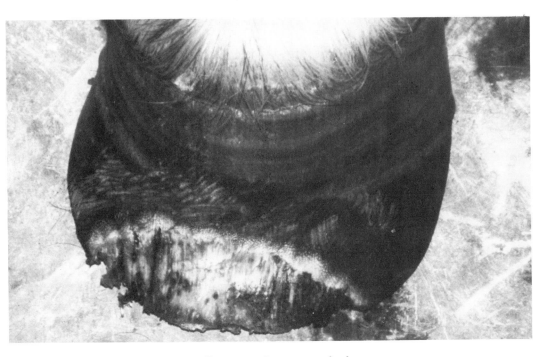

Fig 85 *The dorsal hoof wall partially removed to expose dead*
laminar tissue beneath.

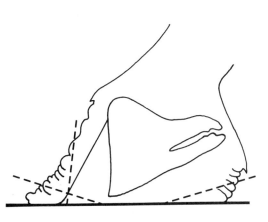

Fig 86 *Trimming the foot of the*
laminitic horse.

requires the full expertise of veterinary surgeon and farrier working with complete co-operation over a prolonged period. In addition, considerable time will be necessary for nursing. It must be understood from the outset that such dedication will be both time-consuming and expensive, and may be unrewarding. In severe cases the humanitarian aspect of such treatment should also be considered before the decision to start treatment is made.

Traditionally it has been the custom to treat cases of laminitis by re-shaping the hoof capsule to realign it with the rotated bone inside. This has been done by shortening the toe so that during walking the leverage of the hoof wall is reduced, and by lowering the heels so that they take more weight (*see* Fig 86). This may not be advisable, however, since, by lowering the heels, further tension is

113

placed on the deep flexor tendon so that rotation of the pedal bone is increased.

Rotation occurs because the structures providing major support within the hoof are lost, so that support of the pedal bone must be provided. This can best be done by fitting a heart bar shoe over the frog so that pressure is applied to support the underside of the pedal bone, but the position in which it is applied is critical. If sole is compressed between the pedal bone and the point of the bar, it will be destroyed, with disastrous consequences. Pressure must therefore be restricted to the frog. If it is applied too near to the heels it will be behind the fulcrum in the centre of the distal interphalangeal joint, around which the pedal bone rotates, and

will worsen the rotation. Conversely, if the pressure is applied too far forward it will compromise the blood-supply to the sole.

The correct position to site the point of the bar is usually approximately one centimetre back from the point of the frog. The bar is sloped upward from heel to toe to increase the pressure under the pedal bone. The amount of pressure to be applied must be assessed empirically to allow more comfortable movement. Too much will increase the level of pain and too little will fail to prevent rotation or give support. Once the correct pressure has been applied the horse should stand happily on the shod foot while the opposite foot is raised. Clearly no form of pain

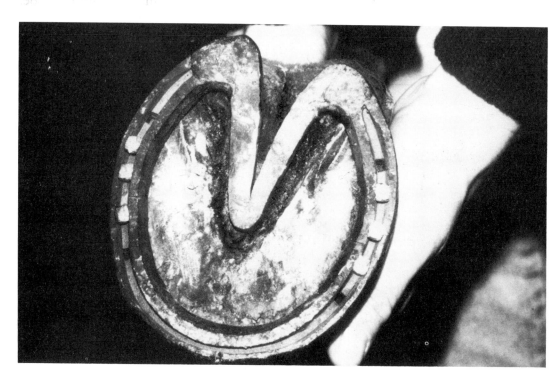

Fig 87 *The heart bar shoe must not extend beyond the extremities of the frog when the heart bar shoe is applied.*

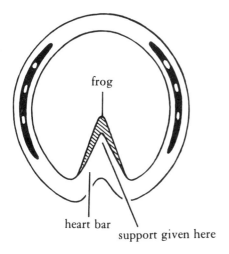

frog

heart bar

support given here

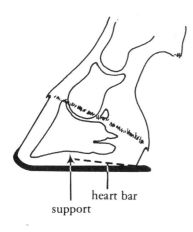

heart bar

support

Fig 88   Heart bar shoe.

suppression can be used while the shoes are being fitted.

The toe is rolled to allow movement with minimum strain on the deep flexor tendon. The shoe is seated out so that no pressure is exerted on the sole. The centre of weight-bearing can be shifted back-wards by the combination of a heart bar and egg bar shoe so that less weight is passed through the pedal bone. This must be beneficial, and the use of a combined

heart and egg bar shoe is worthy of consideration. The egg bar will help to prevent the contraction at the heels that inevitably follows the use of a heart bar shoe. There may also be an indication for the application of heart bar shoes without positive pressure on the bar as a preven-tative measure before rotation of the pedal bone actually occurs. This, too, is not a commonly used procedure.

The feet should be trimmed and the shoes reset at least every three to four weeks since, as the hoof grows, the shoe moves downwards and pressure on the frog reduces. Where it is not practical to reset the shoes frequently enough it is possible to fit a screw adjustment to the bar so that pressure can be altered with-out the necessity of removing the shoe.

In the case of the sinker the shoe is used to brace the whole bony column against the hoof wall to prevent the hoof wall from sliding upwards (*see* Fig 89). The entire force is applied against the nails in the shoe and the maximum skills of the farrier are required if this is to have any chance of being successful.

Where the toe has become elongated and there is a large degree of separation between hoof wall and pedal bone, with debris forcing the two apart, the original foot conformation will not be recovered until the debris is removed. This can be achieved by completely removing a sec-tion of the hoof wall from the toe region, from ground surface to the point where normal laminar attachment is restored, at the coronary band if necessary. The section of wall removed may comprise up to 40 per cent of the total wall. If this is done the sole must then be supported by a heart bar shoe. The exposed tissue should be painted regularly with antiseptic and can be dressed if required. When

115

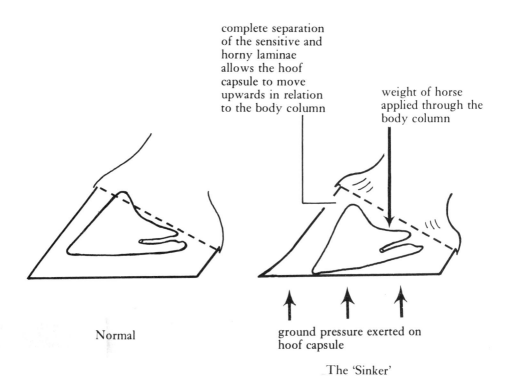

complete separation of the sensitive and horny laminae allows the hoof capsule to move upwards in relation to the body column

weight of horse applied through the body column

Normal

ground pressure exerted on hoof capsule

The 'Sinker'

Fig 89   Sinking of the bony column.

indicated, all four feet can be treated in this radical manner, but such treatment must be managed only by a farrier and a veterinary surgeon experienced in the technique. Where the remaining hoof wall is inadequate to support nails, screws can often be used successfully. The hoof regrows remarkably quickly once the jamming effect at the toe has been relieved, so that the deficit has completely grown out within six months of the resection.

It is helpful in the early stages of treatment to reduce the blood-pressure as much as possible. This can be helped by withholding salt from the diet and feeding 30g daily of potassium chloride. Ground limestone is also helpful in providing calcium in the diet. Methionine is valuable as a feed supplement for the first

month to provide a strong bond in the new laminae as they are formed.

Occasionally laminitis occurs as a sequel to physical damage to the hoof and laminae. This may result from excessive work on a hard surface, in which case both forefeet are likely to be affected, or from a blow to the hoof as may occur when a fence is hit hard during jumping. In this case usually only one foot is affected. Although traumatic laminitis is more likely to occur in the heavier horse and therefore to be more difficult to treat, treatment is exactly the same as for laminitis from all other causes.

Seedy toe, as already described, often follows laminitis. As the normal hoof growth is resumed the defect will gradually grow out. A wide-webbed shoe will protect the damaged white line and

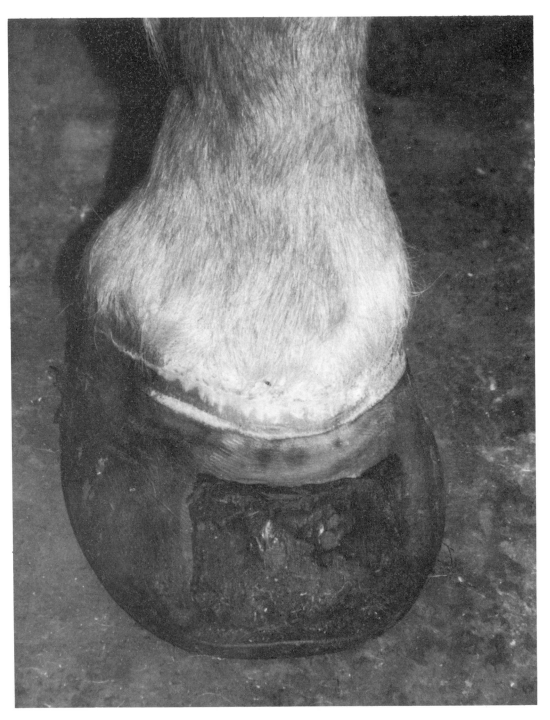

Fig 90   The appearance of the foot several weeks after resection
of the hoof wall.

serve to spread the weight over the hoof wall. Where the damage is extensive the hoof wall can be resected in the same way as for laminitis cases, until the whole affected area has been exposed.

Navicular Disease

Navicular disease is a chronic disease which causes progressive degeneration of one or, more usually, both fore distal sesamoid (navicular) bones. It is a disease primarily of hunters and hacking horses in the age range between five and ten years. It is rare in ponies and Arab horses.

The underlying cause appears to result from damage to the blood-supply to the bone, resulting in lack of nutrition and subsequent degeneration of the bone. The cause is, however, subject to debate. The cartilaginous surfaces become eroded and cavities form in the underlying bone, mainly along the lower border and wings. An increase in cone-shaped spaces along the surface indicates an increase in compensatory blood supply. Such compensation must be due to pathological changes which may not have been identified. In addition, spurs of new bone may extend from the wings, representing damage due to tearing of the attached suspensory ligaments. Reduced blood-supply to the cartilaginous surface leads to increased rate of wear of the cartilage and damage to the overlying deep digital

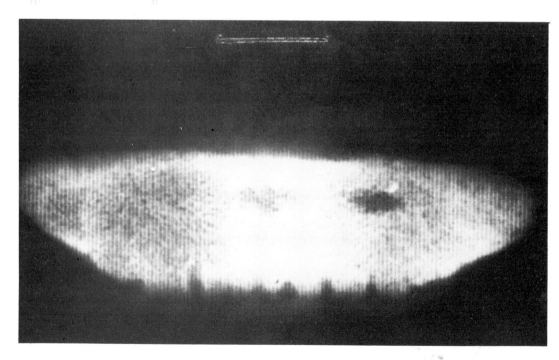

Fig 91 Dark marks on the radiograph of a navicular bone denote areas of bone destruction which may indicate navicular disease.

flexor tendon where it runs over the cartilage.

It is commonly considered that navicular disease is hereditary in nature. This is not so, although navicular disease is more common in horses with a specific conformation and it is this which may be hereditary. The horse with a small foot will apply greater pressure per unit area on that foot than the same horse with a larger foot. Long upright pasterns predispose to the condition, as do long toes and low heels. Long toes are often the long term result of poor shoeing. When the toe is not dressed back sufficiently and a shoe is fitted that is too short at the heels, the heels will not be supported and, over a period of months or years will collapse inwards, putting pressure on the underlying structures including the navicular bone. In addition, the long toe and the broken back hoof/pastern axis will increase tension on the deep digital flexor tendon and on the navicular bone which acts as a pulley for the tendon to change direction. The blood-supply to the bone is reached via the joint capsule. Whereas the capsule above the navicular bone is long, that on the underside is short and easily torn. Consequently the blood-supply to the underside is easily compromised. Over-extension of the joint, as occurs in the heavy horse show jumping on a hard surface, will increase the tearing. Horses that are irregularly worked have a less efficient blood circulation around the foot than do regularly working horses, where the movement acts as an aid to circulation. Tearing of blood-vessels results in increased blood clotting in the tiny capillaries supplying the bone.

Navicular disease is usually insidious in onset. The affected horse is ill at ease when standing and may push the lame foot out in front to reduce the pressure on the heel area, adopting a stance known as 'pointing'. As the lame leg becomes increasingly painful more work is done with the opposite leg, more pressure is applied and in time that, too, becomes affected. The horse will then stand shifting its weight from one foot to the other as with laminitis. Once the horse is walked, however, the gait is seen to be completely different from that of the laminitic horse. The stride is shortened and the toe hits the ground first. In the early stages of the disease the lameness quickly wears off with exercise but as it progresses the period required before soundness is achieved becomes longer. The lameness may be shifting, appearing to be in one leg at one examination and in the other at the next. Often the long toe and shortened stride cause the horse to stumble.

Occasionally lameness may be acute in onset in a horse with navicular disease. Lameness will occur actually during exercise on these occasions and be quite acute in nature. This scenario is more frequent in horses that are regularly exercised.

Close examination of the foot reveals a long toe which may be worn excessively. Sometimes bruising is present at the toe and leads the observer to believe that this is the cause of lameness although, if it were, the horse would place its heel first during movement. Lack of support, the result of poor shoeing, and lack of pressure on the heels, due to the horse's mode of action, lead in the long term to contraction, elongation and inward collapse of the heels, and shrinking of the frog to produce an upright boxy foot. The boxy foot is the product and not the cause of navicular disease.

When pressure is applied to the centre of the frog, immediately over the navicular bone, the horse with navicular disease will usually flinch. Furthermore if the leg is flexed from the pastern downwards for a minute before the horse is trotted away, it will show severe and persistent lameness. Similarly, if the joints are over-extended increased lameness will often be seen.

Apart from the shape of the feet and the response to flexion tests, confirmation of navicular disease relies on three further criteria, all of which must be present. These are:

1.   The horse must have a forelimb lameness with the characteristic action described. Often lameness is present to varying degrees in both forelimbs.
2.   Characteristic changes in the navicular bone must be demonstrable by X-radiography. These changes include cone, lollipop-shaped or branched channels from the lower surface of the navicular bone. Spikes of new bone may also project from its surfaces. Mild degenerative changes may be present in horses that are not lame. Although such findings must be regarded with caution, the horse with no other abnormal signs cannot be considered to have navicular disease and it is difficult to tell whether it is more likely to develop the condition in the future.
3.   There must be some improvement in action when the nerve supply to the heel area is blocked out, although for a variety of reasons the horse may not go completely sound. Once the whole foot is blocked out, lameness may be further reduced. Sometimes adhesions between the navicular bone and the deep flexor tendon physically prevent the horse from having a normal gait. Often when one foot is blocked out the horse will show lameness on the other since lameness in this foot, while having been present all the time, has been masked by the more severe lameness in the opposite foot.

The treatment of navicular disease takes a variety of forms, both medical and surgical. The easiest but least satisfactory line of treatment is to maintain the horse on pain-relieving medical treatment. This has the drawback that it makes no attempt to improve the underlying condition, it is expensive in the long term and horses on such treatment are ineligible to compete under Jockey Club or FEI rules.

Alternative currently acceptable forms of medical treatment are directed at increasing the blood-supply to the navicular bone. Warfarin (Dicoumarol) is used to reduce the blood clots that form in the tiny blood-vessels and block them. Warfarin 'thins' the blood so that it flows more easily. The effect can be easily monitored by checking the time that treated blood samples take to clot compared with the time before treatment began. Although it has the advantage that this treatment is cheap and effective, it has the disadvantage that overdosage can be easily achieved with serious consequences. As a result the effect must be regularly monitored by checking blood samples at least twice a week initially. Furthermore, great care must be taken with regard to the use of any other drugs in combination with this treatment and, theoretically at least, the treatment must be continued on a daily basis indefinitely. In practice, treatment can often be halted after a year or more.

Isoxsuprine is used to dilate the blood-vessels to increase the blood flow to the bone. It is intended that after a single course of treatment the horse will return to full soundness and remain sound. Sometimes a further short course is re- quired after approximately a year to 'boost' the initial effect. The drug is given as a feed supplement for approximately three weeks, at the end of which time the dose is gradually tailed off. It does not require regular monitoring and after the initial treatment a cure should be effected, although the drug is expensive.

Until recently, surgical treatments have been directed towards destroying the nerve supply to the navicular bone so that pain is no longer appreciated. This procedure has numerous potential complications which render it best avoided. A recently developed approach involves the surgical sectioning of the collateral navicular suspensory ligaments and has produced promising results. The ligaments run from each end and the proximal border of the navicular bone, spiralling upwards round the pastern to join the collateral ligaments of the pastern joint. Their function is to raise the back margin of the navicular bone, keeping the joint capsule below the bone under tension. Cutting the ligaments relaxes the tension on the joint capsule and the blood supply through it is consequently increased.

All the forms of treatment described benefit from the concurrent use of remedial shoeing to correct the foot conformation. Efforts can be made to help the contracted heel to expand, either by sloping the heel of the shoe downwards towards the outside (slippering), or by grooving the hoof wall. The slippered shoe is sloped on the bearing surface from inside to outside so that the hoof wall tends to slide outwards. Grooving in-

volves the scoring of vertical lines down the horn of the heel from coronet to ground surface to allow for expansion.

In the early stages of navicular disease, when the hoof/pastern axis is broken back and the heels are weak and low, the centre of the support must be moved as far towards the heels as possible. This can be achieved by using an egg bar shoe which provides support back behind the bulbs of the heels. Clearly the type of exercise that can be undertaken while such shoes are fitted is limited. Where the hoof/pastern axis is broken back corrective trimming should be encouraged, where necessary, by trimming the hoof wall from coronary band to ground surface.

Sesamoiditis

Sesamoiditis is the condition in which one or both of the proximal sesamoid bones at the fetlock become inflamed. Strictly speaking, navicular disease is a distal sesamoiditis but normally the term sesamoiditis is restricted to damage to the proximal sesamoid bones behind the fetlock.

The condition is characterised by simultaneous degeneration of the normal bone, together with new bone proliferation on the surface. Most commonly occurring in the young adult horse between two and five years of age, it is most likely to be found in hunters, jumpers and racehorses, causing a variable degree of lameness which is more pronounced during work on a hard surface.

As is the case with navicular disease, damage results from impaired blood-supply to the bone, usually as the result of a strain to the fetlock joint. Such a strain,

121

due to over-extension of the joint, causes tearing at the apex of the sesamoid where the suspensory ligament is attached, or at the base where the distal sesamoidean ligament attaches. Tearing causes new bone to proliferate at these sites.

Sesamoiditis may be a sequel to disease within the fetlock joint, but this involves the surface of the sesamoid adjacent to the fetlock joint and is not normally regarded as true sesamoiditis.

Where the bone has become wasted the change is irreversible. Prominent enlarged channels within the bone harbour enlarged blood-vessels, following thrombosis within the vessels. Although heat may be present within the damaged fetlock, swelling tends to be minimal. If the leg is supported and pressure applied to the sesamoids a response to pain is evident. The affected horse is unwilling to flex its fetlock fully. If force is used to flex it before the horse is trotted away, lameness will be increased.

The changes that occur during sesamoiditis can be demonstrated X-radiographically but lameness may be present several weeks before the changes can be seen. Consequently, X-radiographs that are taken too early may fail to demonstrate the changes.

It is wise to be cautious in predicting the outcome with regard to the horse's return to future full work. Reduction of the inflammation with cold applications and anti-inflammatory medicines must be followed by a prolonged period of complete rest. This can be achieved by immobilising the lower half of the limb in a plaster cast. Pain to the area can be reduced by removing the nerve supply to the fetlock but such procedures render the horse insufficiently sure-footed to be safe for riding, and are best avoided.

Tendon and Ligament Injuries

Flexor Tendons and Suspensory Ligaments

The superficial and deep flexor tendons and the suspensory ligament act in conjunction with the sesamoid bones and the sesamoidean ligaments to support the fetlock joint. The main function of this joint is to absorb concussion when the weight of the horse comes on to the foot during locomotion. The flexor tendons and suspensory ligament act as shock absorbers. Both to the naked eye and microscopically tendons and ligaments appear very similar. Indeed, the suspensory ligament is a vestigial tendon. Consequently the injuries sustained are similar, as are the treatments.

The function of ligaments is to supply support to joints by restricting movement beyond a certain maximum. To achieve this they are attached to bone on each side of a joint. Tendons, however, control movement of a joint since one end is attached to bone but the other end is attached to muscle which is able to contract and cause the joint to move. Both tendons and ligaments comprise bundles of fibres made up of fibrils of the protein collagen. They run longitudinally down the leg and have a limited degree of elasticity. This means that they have the ability to stretch and to return to their original length. Stretching is made possible by the fact that the resting ligament or tendon is crimped into a zigzag. As tension is applied to the structure the crimping is pulled straight. If tension is applied beyond this, the fibres rupture and the fibre pattern will be lost.

The muscles to which the tendons are attached are situated above the knee and hock so that minimal bulk and weight are attached to the lower limb and hindrance to movement is minimised. One of the setbacks to this arrangement is that the lower limb consists primarily of bone, tendon and ligament, covered by little more than skin and left vulnerable to physical damage.

The blood supply to the tendon comes from the paratenon which surrounds the tendon as a sheath, and is a much better blood supply than is commonly believed. When tendon is damaged, fibroblast cells within the tendon become active in producing new collagen. Unfortunately the type III collagen that is produced as a response to injury is less elastic and not as strong as the original type I collagen, and is more likely to be damaged again.

When damage results from a bandage being applied too tightly to the tendon it is restricted to swelling around the fibres and usually there is no damage to the fibres themselves. Recovery from this sort of injury is rapid and complete. Trauma to the structure from the outside, as may occur after an over-reach or over-extension, causes more serious damage. Tendon strain or trauma is much more common in the forelimb than the hind since most weight is applied to the fore-limbs, particularly when the horse is moving rapidly forward. The horse jumping at speed, the National Hunt horse or eventer, is most vulnerable to damage. Where the pastern is long and sloping or the knee joint is not vertical but 'back at the knee' the likelihood of damage is further increased.

Most of the concussive shock during landing is absorbed by the muscle attached to the tendon. Normally the muscle is relaxed as the foot hits the ground but quickly tenses to absorb the weight. Little sudden change in the tension of the tendon is made so that damage is not normally done. However, if the foot does not hit the ground at the anticipated time due to the surface being uneven, or the surface is harder than anticipated or the muscle is too tired to function properly, more load is placed on the tendon and injury is likely to result. Tiredness results from inadequate preparation for the degree of exertion that is required. The requirement is particularly large in heavy going. If the blood-supply to the tissues is restricted with tight bandages or boots, the damage may be increased.

Trauma may result from chronic or momentary over-use of the structure. Where injury is the result of an external blow, the site of injury is generally more discrete. When the tendon or ligament becomes damaged, the damage is fairly obvious except in the most minor of cases, by the local heat and swelling. In more severe cases it may be difficult to be sure which structures actually are involved. When the knee is flexed to take the horse's weight off the structures, abnormality is more obvious. The actual tendon or ligament feels soft at the site of damage. It is very important that this condition be differentiated from swelling around the tendon arising from a local infection, most frequently spreading from infection within the foot. Enlargement of the vein running adjacent to the flexor tendons down the inside of the leg may also be confused with tendon damage. In this case the vessel becomes more obvious in the flexed leg, and the response of pain when squeezed that is normally found where the tendon is

123

damaged is absent.

Ultrasonic scanning can be used to create a picture of a cross-section through the tendons and ligaments at a given level so that damage within the structures can be visualised. Areas of blood or accumulations of tissue fluids are seen as black areas and the uniform pattern of the fibres is seen to be disrupted. Scanning is very valuable in predicting the time scale that may be required before the horse can be returned to work. Regular scanning can be used to monitor progress.

Damage to the superficial flexor tendon is more common than damage to the deep tendon. *Any* damage is serious. The most common site of injury is in the middle of the cannon where the cross-sectional area of the tendon is least and the strain on the tendon is greatest. Occasionally damage is at the fetlock level, while damage to the deep flexor tendon is most often at this level or lower.

In cases of severe flexor tendon damage the fetlock may become dropped slightly. If the superficial tendon is ruptured the fetlock will be markedly dropped. In cases in which both the superficial and deep flexor tendons are ruptured, the fetlock will sink nearly to the ground and the toe will point into the air. Similarly, when the extensor tendons are ruptured the horse will not be able to extend the toe and will 'knuckle over' on it. With practice the horse learns to flick the toe forward and apply weight quickly to the foot, after which full weight can easily be borne on the damaged leg.

The suspensory ligament arises at the back of the knee and runs immediately behind the cannon as a broad flat band, dividing two thirds of the way down its length and each division attaching to a proximal sesamoid bone at the back of the

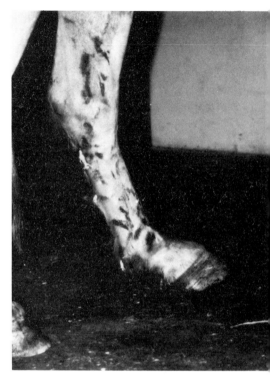

Fig 92 Severe damage to the superficial and deep flexor tendons causes the fetlock to sink and the toe to rise.

fetlock joint. The divisions then pass around the pastern to attach to the common digital extensor tendon (long digital extensor in the hind limb).

Injuries occur in the fore or hind limbs most frequently in one or both of the branches above the sesamoids and result from a short or prolonged period of unequal loading on the two sides. Again the injury is particularly common in horses working at speed, occurring after excessive stretching as the fetlock drops. It is exacerbated by working on rough surfaces or by improper foot balance.

The degree of lameness experienced following injury is variable but is most severe on soft going. Often the pain and

Fig 93 This radiograph of the fetlock illustrates the manner in which the proximal sesamoid bones are pulled towards the foot when the suspensory ligament ruptures.

swelling are delayed in onset but, except in very mild cases, swelling is obvious. It is important to examine the leg radiographically to assess any damage to the related bony structures, particularly the proximal sesamoids from which the suspensory ligament may become detached.

If both branches of the ligament are torn the fetlock becomes dropped slightly. In the event of rupture of the branches there is a marked change in the position of the fetlock. These changes result from over-extension of the fetlock joint at speed and are often accompanied by damage to the flexor tendons. Damage

to the body of the suspensory ligament is less common and is usually associated with damage to adjacent bony structures, notably the splint bones.

When the proximal (top) end of the suspensory ligament is damaged diagnosis is difficult since there is a high concentration of structures in this area, damage to any of which produces similar clinical signs. In these cases the horse is not more lame on soft going but lameness is increased when the affected leg is on the outside during circling.

It is important that damage to all tendons and ligaments is detected as early as possible and that the horse be completely rested after injury. Some opinion suggests that when two weeks have elapsed after the injury, light walking may help to correct alignment of the repair tissue by applying mild stress to the damaged tendon or ligament. This theory has not been adequately tested and requires that the difficult distinction be drawn between appropriate and excessive tension.

Where damage is marked, recovery will often take a year or more. In the first two weeks after injury vigorous attempts to reduce the swelling will pay dividends by minimising the disorganisation of the fibre pattern. Cold applications, together with anti-inflammatory drugs should be accompanied by support. A support bandage must be changed at least twice a day. In cases of severe damage a cast can be used, but it is heavy and often difficult to manage. A support bandage is also helpful on the opposite leg.

After the initial phase of repair has subsided, which will take a period of approximately three to four weeks, it has been customary to fire or surgically split the damaged tendon or ligament. The

125

argument runs that by introducing heat to the tendon at a time when the acute inflammatory response is subsiding, the inflammation will be renewed and more rapid healing occurs. Unfortunately the technique used inevitably creates far more damage within the tendon. Furthermore the scar tissue that results from this type of repair is of type III collagen, which is much less strong than the original type I collagen. Evidence suggests that these procedures do not in fact increase the rate of repair and that tendon splitting may actually slow the repair. Tendon splitting may be more successful when used on the suspensory ligament since movement of the ligament is minimal, and adhesions formed with surrounding structures are less important. Implantation of carbon fibre into the tendon induces the tendon to create its own type I collagen, but usually involves a tendon-splitting operation to accurately place the implant.

Laser and ultrasonic treatment of damaged tendons and ligaments accelerate reduction of the acute inflammation but it is unlikely that they increase the overall rate of healing.

Where the fetlock joint is seriously dropped as the result of injury it is probably advisable to surgically fix it, although an animal thus treated is useful only for breeding. Early cases of complete tendon and ligament laceration can be surgically repaired on some occasions by stitching the severed ends together.

Following severe damage the horse should be box rested for at least three months, while on a minimal diet. If the horse is turned out to recover during this time it can generally be assumed that the recovery time will be doubled. When the horse is returned to work the return

Fig 94   The appearance of the legs following pin firing.

should be gradual and slow. Horses in which there is a change in position of the fetlock are unlikely to ever again be capable of fast work.

It has been traditional in cases of tendon or ligament damage to apply a Patten shoe. This shoe raises the heels of the foot by extending the heels vertically downward and joining them by a bar, thereby resting the back of the leg. The purpose is to reduce the tension on the deep flexor tendon that is attached to the solar surface of the pedal bone. In practice the value of the shoe has been equivocal. This may be because the injury contracts as it repairs so that if tension is removed from the tendon or ligament the structure repairs too short, so that further stress is applied

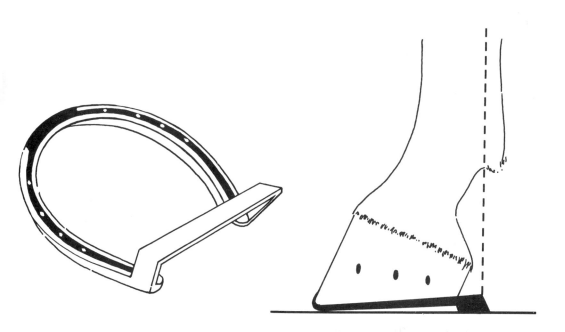

Fig 95   The Patten or rest shoe.

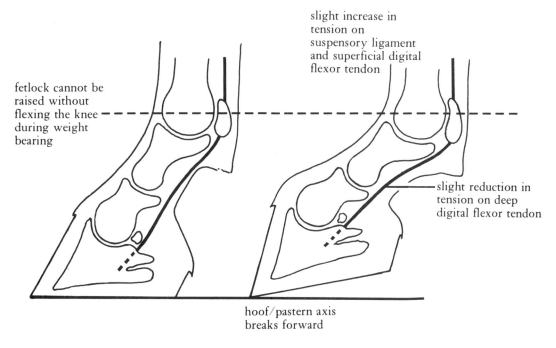

slight increase in
tension on
suspensory ligament
and superficial digital
flexor tendon

fetlock cannot be
raised without
flexing the knee
during weight
bearing

slight reduction in
tension on deep
digital flexor tendon

hoof/pastern axis
breaks forward

Fig 96   Mechanical effect of raising the heel.

when the normal shoe is re-applied. An alternative explanation is that although the heel is raised and the pedal bone is rotated, when weight is applied to the leg the raised heel must be compensated by dropping the fetlock further, so that the tension on the deep flexor tendon is not significantly reduced (*see* Fig 96).

If the toe is long, leverage on the toe is increased, thereby increasing tension on the deep flexor tendon. To avoid this it is important to ensure that the toe is kept well trimmed to minimise the effect. By extending the shoes backward to the level of the fetlock or beyond, support will be given to the fetlock by shifting the centre of gravity backwards (*see* Fig 97). The farther the point of attachment of the shoe (the nails) is from the fetlock, the greater the tearing effect, so that a short foot is valuable in reducing the tension on the nails. In this respect an egg bar shoe would be of great value in supplying support to the leg.

Where there is complete rupture of one or more of the flexor tendons or suspensory ligament and sinking of the fetlock, a shoe that supports the fetlock is very valuable. The heels of the shoe are extended upward and joined by a sling beneath the fetlock. This provides direct support to the fetlock without placing strain on the nails of the shoe.

It should be remembered that any shoe projecting well beyond the foot is likely to become tangled in straw and this form of bedding is best avoided.

Whatever treatment is given, damage to tendons and ligaments requires a prolonged recovery period. Early recognition of damage and conscientious nursing are extremely important but active steps can be taken, at least in part, to avoid damage.

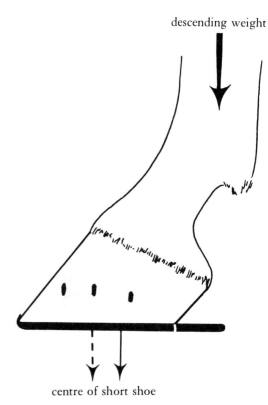

descending weight

centre of short shoe

extending the shoes moves the centre backwards, towards the point lying directly beneath the weight descending through the limb

Fig 97 Support supplied to the back of the leg by lengthening the shoe.

The achievement of full fitness will maximise the horse's co-ordination for a longer period of time so that abnormal stresses are not placed on the structures. It is probably advisable to avoid the use of tightly-fitting boots since they may, by constriction, reduce the blood-supply to the tendons and ligaments. Finally the shape of the foot should be considered. By avoiding the long foot with low heels and ensuring a normal hoof/pastern axis, the tension applied to the flexor tendons and suspensory ligaments is minimised.

Curbs

The small swelling that occurs immediately below the point of the hock, at the back where it joins the cannon bone is commonly called a curb. It is particularly common in young horses and is best seen from one side when the hock is in profile. Such a swelling constitutes damage to the plantar ligament that runs vertically down the caudal (back) surface of the hock joint and an enlargement of the underlying fibular tarsal bone. Although it is present most commonly in the horse with sickle hocks, it may also result from excessive flexion of the joint as the horse comes to a rapid halt, or from trauma from kicking walls or the tail ramp of a trailer.

Only in the early acute stage is lameness generally present, when the horse stands with the heel elevated and heat and swelling around the plantar ligament. If complications such as local infection or new bone formation occur, lameness is prolonged. Local scar tissue formation may cause a permanent enlargement but no pain.

During the painful phase, relief may be provided by raising the heel of the foot using a wedge between shoe and heel.

Developmental Abnormalities in Tendons and Ligaments

Contracted Tendons

The term contracted tendons is something of a misnomer since tendons have a very limited ability to contract. A few horses suffer severe traumatic injury to the tendons in which contraction does take place during healing but in the majority of cases the deformity arises through abnormal growth of tendons and their attached muscle, and ligaments. The growth is insufficient in these cases to keep pace with the growth of the bone to which they are adjacent.

Contracted tendons fall into two categories, those that are congenital and arise at or soon after birth, and those that are acquired. All, however, occur within the first year or so of life when bone growth is most rapid.

The condition of congenital contracted tendons is usually attributed to the foal's lying in the wrong position within the womb but it appears that other factors are often involved. Influential factors may include a genetic component or contact by the pregnant mare with poisonous agents or infections. Usually the evidence for this is circumstantial. Either one or several limbs may be affected but it is usually most serious in the forelimbs, causing knuckling of the fetlock when both deep and superficial flexor tendons are involved, or the coffin joint when only the deep tendon is affected. Shortening may be so severe that the animal walks on the anterior surface of the foot.

Commonly only the knee is flexed and these cases are associated with relative

129

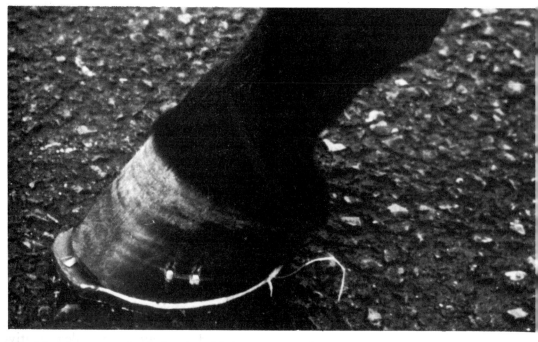

Fig 98 *A toe extension is fitted to aid the treatment of contracted tendons.*

contracture of the supporting ligaments on the surface behind the knee joint. All contractions may be associated with rotational deformity.

The great majority of congenital deformities resolve themselves spontaneously within a few weeks; others may require splinting. Plastic guttering with judiciously placed padding is ideal for this. Casting is best kept as a final resort since casts tend to create severe management problems. The application of a shoe with an extension at the toe is useful to straighten the foot. Unlike the treatment used for acquired cases of contracted tendons, corrective surgery is rarely necessary.

Acquired contracted tendons may affect one or both forelegs and involve fetlock or coffin joints. One cause is natural flexion of a painful limb for a prolonged period. The muscle attached

Fig 99 *The shoe with toe extension (ground surface).*

Fig 100   Clubbed foot due to relatively short deep flexor tendon.

to the tendon becomes contracted and remains so after the initial cause of pain has gone. Alternatively, overfeeding or feeding imbalance may predispose to the problem. Excessive energy and, possibly, protein intake causes rapid bone growth with which tendon and ligament growth cannot compete. If exercise is restricted there is no tendency to stretch the structures. The check ligament below the knee is unable to lengthen adequately, further shortening the deep digital flexor tendon (DDFT).

When the DDFT is involved the coffin joint is held flexed and the horse develops a rotated pedal bone and upright clubbed foot. Although this can resemble laminitis radiographically in that the toe of the pedal bone is pulled into a more vertical position, unlike in laminitis the

upper (dorsal) surface of the pedal bone remains in line with the dorsal hoof wall. In severe cases the bone may extend beyond the vertical. If no effort is made to correct the condition the horse will develop a joint degeneration in the coffin joint and ultimately the tapered tip of the pedal bone will be squared off to support the horse's weight. Correction must be rapid. Although clubbed foot normally occurs in younger horses, it may develop at twelve months of age or more.

Flexion at the fetlock normally occurs in the older foal and is associated with shortening of both deep and superficial flexor tendons. It is important to identify which tendons and ligaments are involved before treatment can commence. Again, delay may result in degenerative damage to the joint. The position of the hoof on the ground is normal.

As with congenital cases, many affected horses can be corrected by conservative treatment involving trimming of the heels to allow more tension to be applied to the shortened structures, together with a severe reduction in diet and increase in exercise. In addition, a shoe with a toe extension will help, by its leverage action, to force the heels on to the ground.

Where the fetlock is contracted, the use of wedges to raise the heel causes the fetlock to drop, applying greater tension on its supporting structures. This produces good results.

Surgery is far more likely to be necessary in cases of acquired contraction. In mild cases involving the coffin joint, cutting the carpal check ligament that attaches the DDFT behind the knee allows the tendon to drop sufficiently to produce an immediate response. If a shoe is applied with a toe extension the results

131

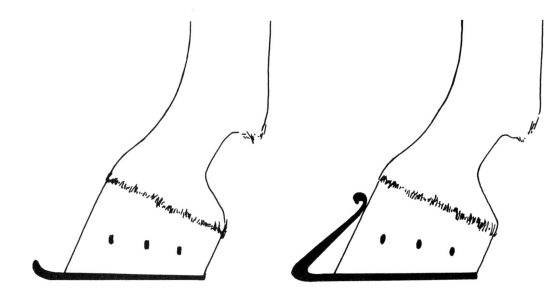

Fig 101   Toe extension shoe for treatment of 'contracted tendon'.

are good even in some severe cases. In those that are not successful, the DDFT must be cut. This seriously restricts the horse's future functional life and may be cosmetically unacceptable, depending on the site at which the surgery is performed.

The results of surgery to the fetlock are less predictable and involve cutting either the superficial flexor tendon or the radial check ligament above the knee.

Joint Extension

The hind limbs of new-born foals are sometimes excessively extended, primarily at the fetlock joints, probably due to inadequate support being provided by the flexor tendons. The hoof wall adopts the curved shape of a rocker and the foal rocks back on its heels. In most cases it is important to trim the bearing surface until it is flat, without removing any toe, so that partial dislocation of the coffin joint is prevented. Radiographic evaluation of each case is essential before corrective action is commenced. Most foals recover within a few days, especially if forced to exercise.

An exaggeration of this condition may result in the foal walking on its pasterns. In these cases the application of shoes in which the heels have been elongated may be helpful, but often it is not and surgery to shorten the flexor tendons is likewise limited in its chance of success.

132

8 Future Trends

As with so many sciences, the approach by both the veterinary surgeon and the farrier to the problem of the lame horse has emerged from a period of latency. It is undergoing a renaissance with a haste that suggests that it is attempting to make up for lost time. This is largely the result of a new co-operation between the veterinary surgeon and farrier and the acceptance, however reluctantly, that some of the very foundations on which shoeing has been based for many years may actually be responsible for causing some of the lower limb lamenesses which are so common in the horse. Such a massive step requires a very open minded approach. As we know, problems in the foot are still by far the most common cause of lameness. The renewed interest is present in all aspects of the identification and the correction of lameness, and in shoeing the sound and the lame horse to achieve maximum comfort and the optimal performance at work.

It has recently been confirmed, to the surprise of many people, that the site of hind limb lameness cannot be identified merely by watching the moving horse, since the gait abnormality is intrinsically the same, irrespective of the site of pain. Furthermore, gait analysis with the naked eye is difficult since subtle gait compensations occur in the lame horse. Even a video camera produces a film with resolution too poor to allow for an accurate diagnosis.

Although gait analysis has been conducted since 1840 when a Frenchman, Marey, made scientific studies, any degree of accurate measurement is recent. With the improvement of high speed cinematographic techniques has come a wealth of new information concerning the gait of the normal horse, compared with that of the lame horse under various conditions. Unfortunately, 16mm cinematography is expensive and very time consuming, but it is a useful research tool when linked to computer analysis to establish a data bank. When used with electrogoniometry it provides a valuable method for monitoring the response to treatment after a diagnosis has been made and treatment begun. (Electrogoniometry is a method of electrically measuring movement in a joint without entering the joint.)

A treadmill can be used as a research tool in gait analysis provided that it can be established that the gait is identical to that on a firm surface. It allows performance to be examined under strictly controlled conditions and is tolerated well by the horse.

Force plates in the ground are used to measure the characteristics of the forces that result when the limb makes contact with the ground. Usually these are measured in a vertical plane and in two dimensions horizontally. When combined with transducers mounted on the hoof wall or shoe it is also possible to measure the forces of impact, and acceleration and deceleration of the foot. By measuring the distortion of the foot they help to evaluate the elasticity and the strength of the hoof wall and the coronary band. The stability of the normal and the abnormal foot with and without shoes can be established. For example, the technique has led us to realise that movement within the foot is very complex. At the point of impact between the foot and the ground a force in excess of 1,000kg comes to a sudden halt in the galloping horse. In the impact the pedal bone moves down and away from the hoof wall and then back towards it. The heart bar shoe provides stability during this process in the normal foot but may be less effective in providing stability in the laminitic foot.

Force transducers alone can be valuable in measuring the deformations of the foot which may occur on varying surfaces, thus facilitating in the design of race tracks which will reduce the traumatic effect on the horse to a minimum.

New techniques are being developed to aid the diagnosis of lameness. Xeroradiography is a type of radiography in which a very high definition picture is obtained, suitable for the identification of small chip fractures in bone, or of stress fractures. Inevitably, the technique is at present prohibitively expensive. Electromyography is establishing a place as a specialised technique to measure electrical activity in muscles. It can be useful in identifying some of the more obscure muscular disorders in the lame horse.

In the laboratory, the joint fluid from damaged joints is being carefully studied to develop techniques by which specific conditions of the joint can be recognised from changes within the fluid. In particular, the possibility is under study of measuring the inflammatory mediators, called eicosanoids, as an indicator of the degree of inflammation within the joint.

If possible it would be helpful to have a marker which would indicate whether the damaged. joint would be likely to recover with rest or whether further damage would be likely to result, in which case treatment could be started at the earliest possible time. Inflammation can be suppressed within the joint using sodium hyaluronate or polysulphated glycosaminoglycan, provided that no infection is present.

Extensive research is in progress to look at the manner in which bones and joints respond to loading. The bone which is not loaded becomes weakened by loss of structure. Even very short periods of loading, provided they are repeated, maintain good bone structure. Joint disease causing degenerative changes is extremely common in horses of all ages, but in most cases the cause or causes have still to be identified.

Much interest has been focused on laminitis as has already been explained in Chapter 7, largely as a result of completely re-examining the condition from first principles and correcting mistakes in the basic tenets. By increasing our understanding of the complaint it has become clear that such a complex condition cannot be treated using a standard technique, but that each case must be carefully assessed before treatment begins. Research is in progress to develop a vaccine against the bacteria that produce the damaging endotoxins that underlie so many episodes of laminitis. With luck, in the future laminitis may become as rare as tetanus.

While medical treatments continue to be developed for lamenesses, surgical techniques keep pace. Much progress has been made in the repair of fractures of the long bones of the lower limbs, sometimes with complete return to full work. In addition, surgical treatment of some joints improves the comfort of the horse. Navicular disease can be treated surgically with a fair degree of success.

At the same time our understanding of the foot leads us to appreciate the importance of good foot care. By carefully considering how to trim and shoe the lame horse, conformation can be improved and the lame horse can be made more comfortable or even sound. In the search for a more effective and comfortable shoe the approach has been changed completely in some instances. Most of the new designs are based on the principle of cushioning using a moulded insert between hoof and shoe to reduce the concussion passing through the foot, or a shoe that acts as a protective cushion over the whole sole. This may be fitted without nails and attached by webbing straps.

Some of these shoes are very long lasting and considerable hoof growth may occur while they are fitted. Furthermore, care must be taken in fitting to ensure that damage does not result from abrasion on the heels. The 'Glue Strider' shoe was designed as a plastic shoe which is glued by tabs on to the hoof wall. This has a useful application in horses in which the horn has become so badly damaged

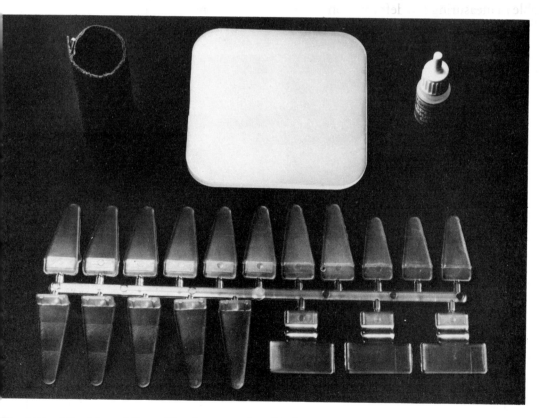

Fig 102   The Mustad Easy-Glu shoe comes in a kit form.

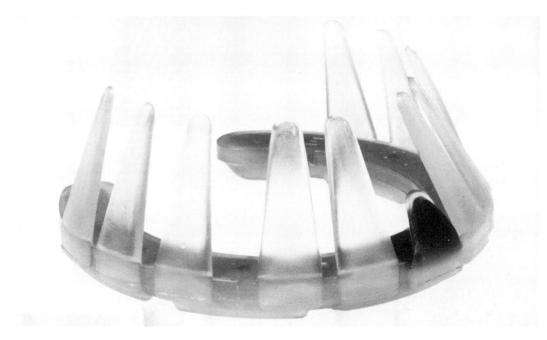

Fig 103   The Easy-Glu shoe.

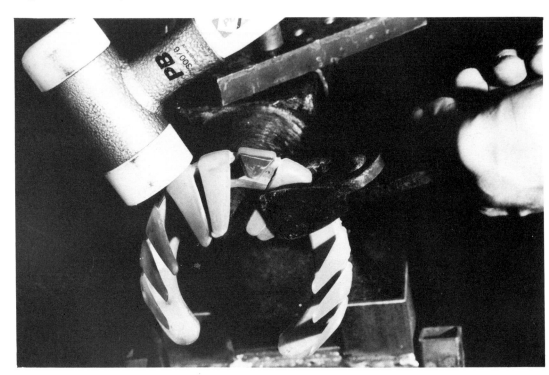

Fig 104   Shaping and forming of the shoe.

136

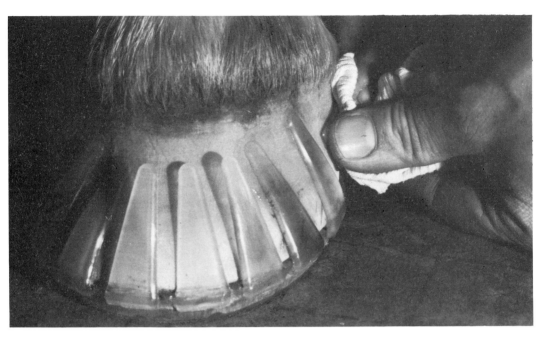

Fig 105 *After careful preparation of the foot and fitting of the shoe, the tabs are then stuck to the outside of the hoof wall.*

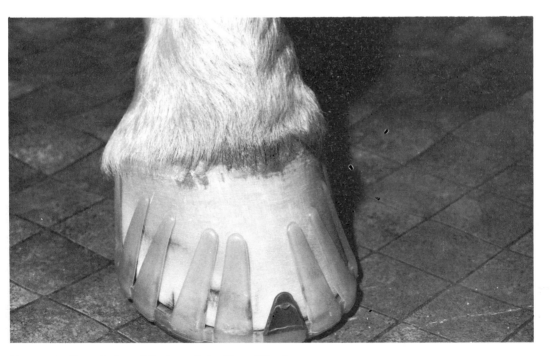

Fig 106 *Completion of fitting of the Easy-Glu shoe.*

that it is unable to support the nails required to hold on a normal shoe. Already a modified version, the Glue II, has superseded the original design and has the advantage of being made entirely from polyurethane. In addition the tabs are supplied separately and can be 'welded' on at the points that suit each foot specifically, using a specialised heat gun. However, this modern innovation is unlikely to replace metal shoes for general use in the near future since it is very slow to fit and very expensive to buy. Of greater value is likely to be the Baby Glu II, which is designed for use with foals. It is much safer than a standard shoe since there is no protuberant metal shoe or nails. Used as one component of a programme for the correction of limb deviations, it is helpful in providing for easy manufacture of extensions at the toe or on the medial or lateral aspects of the foot. The hoof wall is not damaged by frequent alteration or resetting of the shoe as the deviation is corrected.

Poor horn conformation often results from poor blood supply. Perhaps by increasing the blood flow a more resilient horn can be produced. If this were sufficiently resistant to wear it might be possible to dispense with shoes altogether.

Glossary

Afferent nerve   A nerve fibre or tract carrying impulses towards the spinal cord of brain.

Analgesia   The relief of pain without loss of consciousness.

Appendicular   Attached to the trunk, i.e. the limbs.

Arthritis   Inflammation of a joint.

Axial   Along the centre line of the body or part of it.

Bearing surface   Surface adjacent to the ground.

Bilateral   Involving both sides

Bursa   A fluid filled structure between two moving tissues to prevent friction between them.

Calkin   Heel of the shoe turned down on the ground surface to improve grip.

Cancellous bone   Loose bony structure arranged as a three dimensional grating within a long bone.

Capillary   The narrowest of blood vessels. Hairlike.

Carbohydrate   A nutrient substance used to provide energy.

Carpus   The joint of the forelimb between the radius and the metacarpus, commonly called the knee.

Cartilage   Smooth white elastic substance forming the surface of a joint.

Caudal   Pertaining to the tail.

Congenital   Present from the time of birth.

Cranial   Pertaining to the head.

Digit   Portion of limb below the fetlock, the toe.

Dishing   Circular motion of the lower limb during movement.

Distal   Farthest from the body.

Dorsal   On the front or upper surface.

Efferent nerve   A nerve fibre of tract carrying impulses away from the spinal cord or brain.

Epidermis   The outer layer of skin.

Epiphysis   The end of a long bone separated from the shaft by a plate of cartilage which is responsible for increase in length of the bone.

Fibrocartilage   Form of cartilage with increased tensile strength for use in tendon insertions, for example.

Fullering   The groove running round the ground surface of some shoes.

Keratinization   Compression and toughening of skin to form horn or hoof.

Lateral   On the outside, away from the midline.

Ligament   A dense fibrous structure joining two bones together at a joint.

Medial   On the inside, towards the midline.

Nutrient   Food material providing nourishment.

Ossify   Harden to become bone.

Osteoarthritis   Chronic inflammation of the bones within a joint.

Osteomyelitis   Infection within a bone.

Palmar   On the back of the forelimb.

Periosteum   A dense membrane over the surface of bone.

Phalanx   One of the three supporting bones of the digit.

Plantar   On the back of the hind limb.

Plexus   Network of fibres.

Poultice   A warm soft application increasing the blood supply to the area of the skin to which it is applied.

Proximal Closest to the body.

Safed off Rounded on the outside edge of the bearing surface.

Seated out Lowering of the inside of the foot surface of the shoe to relieve pressure from the sole.

Sesamoid A bone situated adjacent to a muscle or its tendon to assist its passage over a joint.

Splanchnic Pertaining to an internal organ.

Synovial sheath A sheath lubricated by fluid through which a tendon passes.

Tarsus The joint of the hind limb between the tibia and the metatarsal bones, commonly called the hock.

Tendon A dense fibrous structure joining a muscle to bone.

Transducer A device that receives signals in one form and converts them into signals in a different form.

Trauma Injury caused by violence.

Unilateral Involving only one side.

Vascular Having vessels.

Ventral On the lower surface, directed towards the belly.

Index